cahokia
MOUNDS

AMERICA'S FIRST CITY

William Iseminger

THE
History
PRESS

Published by The History Press
Charleston, SC 29403
www.historypress.net

Cover image: Painting of Cahokia Mounds, circa AD 1200. *William R. Iseminger, Cahokia
Mounds State Historic Site.*

Cover design by Natasha Momberger.

First published 2010
Second printing 2010
Third printing 2010
Fourth printing 2011
Fifth printing 2012

ISBN 9781540220271

Library of Congress Cataloging-in-Publication Data

Iseminger, William R.
Cahokia mounds : America's first city / William R. Iseminger.
p. cm.
Includes bibliographical references.
ISBN 978-1-59629-734-0
1. Cahokia Mounds State Historic Park (Ill.) 2. Mississippian culture--Illinois--American
Bottom. 3. Indians of North America--Illinois--American Bottom--Antiquities. 4.
American Bottom (Ill.)--Antiquities. I. Title.
E99.M6815I83 2010
977.3'86--dc22
2009050441

Notice: The information in this book is true and complete to the best of our knowledge. It
is offered without guarantee on the part of the author or The History Press. The author
and The History Press disclaim all liability in connection with the use of this book.

This book is dedicated to Jason, Shelly, Mitchell and Jack Augustin.

Contents

Preface

My "Journey to Cahokia"

My interest in archaeology started when I was a child and my family would visit my father's parents and relatives in Heyworth, Illinois, during some of our vacations. My uncle Wendell Iseminger was an artifact collector, and he would take us kids with him to the cornfields of McLean County to search for Indian artifacts. I guess I knew since about seventh or eighth grade that I wanted to be an archaeologist when I grew up. I would read about the subject whenever I got a chance. I recall one period when I was laid up sick for about a week, I pulled out the volume of *Encyclopedia Americana* that dealt with archaeology and read through that.

Upon graduation from Bishop Denis J. O'Connell High School in Arlington, Virginia, I applied to several universities and had hoped to go to the University of Kentucky with a close friend, Michael Hoffman, who was also going into archaeology (he later became a prominent Egyptologist). However, in some mix-up, my high school transcripts did not get sent to Kentucky, but I did gain acceptance to the University of Oklahoma (OU). Throughout my tenure there, Dr. Robert Bell was my advisor and helped me decide on my courses.

During a vacation break my freshman year, when I was back home in Arlington, my mother suggested I go to the Smithsonian in Washington to get some information about employment in archaeology. I set up an appointment and met with Clifford Evans, the director of the Smithsonian. He informed me about a summer research program they had called the River Basin Survey Project along the Missouri River in South Dakota. I applied for a position on that project and was selected to join it in the summer of 1963. I worked for Jake Hoffman on several sites about thirty miles south of Pierre that were to be inundated by a new lake. It was an interesting summer and my first true field experience.

I did not work in the field again until after I graduated from OU and went to Southern Illinois University–Carbondale (SIUC) for graduate studies in anthropology. In the spring of 1967, my uncle Wendell took me to the Illinois State Museum in Springfield to meet with the director, Milton Thompson, to see if there were any summer employment opportunities. Mr. Thompson told me of the work going on at Dickson Mounds in preparation for the construction of a new museum there. I had visited that fascinating site several times in the past and jumped at the opportunity to work there, which I did during the summer of 1967 as a field hand. We primarily worked in the cemetery area where the new building would have an impact. Several project directors came and went during that summer, including Joseph Caldwell, Robert Hall and Emily Blasingham. Howard Winters was doing research in the lab, and Alan Harn was my field supervisor. It was also there that I met Steve Jenne, who was an assistant field supervisor; we became best friends and remain so today (he was best man at my wedding). Following that summer, Steve and I attended an American Anthropological Association meeting in Washington, D.C. We stayed with his mentor, archaeologist William Gardner, who was teaching at Catholic University. At the meeting, Gardner introduced us to Melvin Fowler from the University of Wisconsin–Milwaukee, who was conducting research at Cahokia, and after talking with him for a while, he said to contact him about working at Cahokia that summer. We did, and we both ended up there in the summer of 1968. Steve worked at Monks Mound, and I worked on the South Stockade excavations. Jim Anderson was my project director, and Wayne Glander was the field supervisor.

While I continued my graduate studies at SIUC, I was director of a couple of research projects: an archaeological survey and excavations in the Kinkaid Creek Valley west of Murphysboro, which was to be dammed and flooded by a lake; and a survey and excavations in the lower thirty miles of the Kaskaskia River Valley, which was being straightened for barge traffic. The Kinkaid research served as my master's project, and the Kaskaskia project was my first publication in archaeology, jointly authored with Michael McNerney.

In the fall of 1970, I attended the annual meeting of the Illinois Archaeological Survey in Champaign and ran into Jim Anderson. He asked what I was doing, and I said I was finishing up my master's and looking for work. He asked if I would like to work at Cahokia, and of course I said yes. He had been offered a position there through the Illinois State Museum as curator for the small museum that had formerly been run by the Department of Conservation in one small room of a building that was once a site manager's dwelling. The ISM and DOC had entered into a joint agreement, with the ISM being responsible for the museum, interpretation and educational program development and DOC managing the grounds. Jim had approval to search for an assistant, so I interviewed with ISM director Milton Thompson (again), and he hired me for that position. I started working at Cahokia full time in April 1971.

The staff expanded the little museum into the whole building, knocking out walls and adding rooms, and eventually we had over thirty exhibits, a small theatre and a gift shop. We also built house reconstructions and experimental gardens. I was involved with East Stockade excavations for most of the years I have been at Cahokia, as well as excavations into Mound 50 and on the Woodhenge with public field schools. With the planning and opening of our new Interpretive Center in 1989, my job duties have changed and are now more museum and administrative oriented, and I only occasionally get to do some archaeology on my own time (including three summers co-directing Earthwatch Institute field schools with colleague John Kelly). My focus has been mostly on public archaeology, and I am in charge of interpretation, exhibits and public relations at Cahokia. It has been a fruitful and fascinating thirty-nine years at this site, and I never had thoughts about going anywhere else. As I often tell people, I guess I've found my niche.

I never fail to be fascinated by Cahokia, and still, every time I climb to the top of Monks Mound, it takes my breath away—both literally and figuratively—and I try to imagine what was here, what happened and what these people who built this ancient city were really like. This is an amazing place with much yet to be learned, and I am proud to be able to be part of its modern history and to produce this book as part of my legacy.

Acknowledgements

There are many people who played roles in my life that led to the publication of this book, including my uncle Wendell Iseminger, who first sparked my interest in artifacts and archaeology in the fields of McLean County, Illinois; my mother, Marion Iseminger, who supported and encouraged me throughout my educational journey and in life in general; my college professors at the University of Oklahoma and Southern Illinois University–Carbondale, who instilled the knowledge critical to the pursuit of an archaeological career; the personnel of the Smithsonian River Basin Survey, the Illinois State Museum and Dickson Mounds Museum, with whom I had my first field experiences; Frank Rackerby and Phil Weigand, who provided the opportunity to direct research in southern Illinois while I was a graduate student; Walter Taylor, who helped me learn how to write with his critical editing; Mike Fowler, who provided my first experience in Cahokia archaeology and helped formulate my understanding of this great site; Jim Anderson, friend and colleague, who brought me to Cahokia in 1971 for my lifetime career here; all of the site managers I have worked for—Anderson, Margaret Brown, Neil Rangen and Mark Esarey—and the direction and freedom they have given me to do my job; all of my co-workers and volunteers at Cahokia over these thirty-nine years, too numerous to mention individually; and the Cahokia Mounds Museum Society, its officers, directors and board members, with whom I have worked closely in many capacities since its founding in 1976.

There are many colleagues in archaeology, besides those mentioned above, whom I have known, been friends with, worked for, collaborated with, been inspired by and even disagreed with, and they should also be recognized. They appear here in no particular order, and you will see many of them referenced throughout this manuscript: John and Cricket Kelly, Terry Norris, James Brown, Bill Woods, Elizabeth Benchley, Tim Pauketat, Brad Koldehoff, George Milner, Alan Harn, Mike Wiant, Barbara Vander Leest, Nelson Reed, George Holley, Rinita Dalan, Mary Beth Trubitt, Robert Hall, Warren Wittry, Neal Lopinot, Ken Williams, T.R. Kidder, Tim Schilling, Gayle Fritz, Jimmy Griffin, Jim Collins, Mike Gregg, Mikels Skele, Bonnie Gums, Joe Harl, Carol Diaz Granados, Jim Duncan, Jon Muller, Bob Salzer, Bonnie Styles, Mary Vermilion, Robin Machiran, Tim Baumann, Chuck Bareis, Tom Emerson, Mike Hoffman, Julie Holt, Bob Gergen, Larry Kinsella, Steve Jenne and many others whom I am sure I am neglecting to mention.

But I especially want to thank my wife, Gloria, for being the invaluable life partner and friend she has been for the past thirty-seven years, tolerating all of my foibles, books and disorderly office, always with a smile. Plus, her thirty-six years as a secretary made her an invaluable editor for my writings, including this book.

Introduction

When I was approached by The History Press to do a book on Cahokia, I was flattered. I had planned for many years to do such a book, probably when I retired, but when this opportunity was presented, I agreed to begin work on it right away. In the past fifteen to twenty years, there have been numerous books written by archaeologists about this fascinating site, and I was wondering what I could do that would be different. Some of those books were re-workings of doctoral theses and involved a lot of theory and technical data. Others were edited volumes covering a wide range of topics relating to Cahokia, its people, technology, material culture, economy, belief systems, trade networks, political structure, settlement patterns and more. Still other books were more general in nature, written for popular consumption with less detail and jargon.

What I decided to do was to blend all of this information into a book that would be written for the general public, who, with little or no knowledge of archaeology and Cahokia, would gain an understanding of the place we call Cahokia, its people and the archaeological research that has provided us with that information. This is not an easy task since there are many perspectives of Cahokia offered by its researchers, ranging from conservative and minimalist views to those that are more liberal in view. Some have more of an environmental and ecological perspective, and others place more emphasis on politics and power. I have tried to reach a balance in my presentation, but I will give indications of alternate views where I think they are important.

Unlike most archaeological books and journals, the text will not be full of citation sources that make for awkward reading, but occasionally I will mention a particular book or article, and one can find that source in the bibliography. I have relied heavily on the writings of certain authors and summarized their views in my own words as much as possible. Some of the information I present is in my own memory bank, from lectures, papers, articles and books I have heard and read over the nearly four decades I have worked at Cahokia, as well as personal communications and discussions with many of my colleagues. My first impressions of Cahokia were heavily influenced by Dr. Melvin Fowler, as I initially worked for him and his colleague, Jim Anderson, at the site. He was the only one who had written much about Cahokia at the time. Since then, the works of John Kelly, Cricket Kelly, Tim Pauketat, George Milner, Bill Woods, Tom Emerson, George Holley, Rinita Dalan, Robert Hall, Mark Mehrer, James Brown and others have allowed me to be aware of other perspectives, alternate views or the expansion of the ideas of Fowler.

What I decided to do with part of this book was to take a more detailed look at some of the site's major features and discuss them more extensively than do most of the general books on Cahokia but with less technicality than some of the books written exclusively about those features. Again, my focus in the book, as in most of my work at Cahokia, is interpreting the site for the general public.

That is one reason I use the conventional BC and AD for dates, as that is what most people understand (even though most realize that BC stands for "Before Christ" but seldom know that AD stands for *Anno Domini*, or "since Christ was born"). Historically that has been the most common system, even in some non-Christian nations. Occasionally I will use BP, for "Before Present," such as 1000 BP, which really means "1000 years ago." I find the new politically correct system of "BCE," or "Before the Common Era," and "CE," for "Common Era," to be very awkward and compromising, as it often has to be explained; besides, everyone knows that it really means BC or AD.

Some chapters will be more lengthy than others since there is much more information to present, especially in the cases of Monks Mound and Mound 72. It was as difficult to decide what to include as it was to decide what to exclude in this book. The many photographs and maps come mostly from the archives at the Cahokia Mounds Interpretive Center, taken by myself and other site staff, and some come from the collections of the Illinois State Museum, the University of Wisconsin–Milwaukee, the Pete Bostrom/Lithic

Casting Lab and a few other sources. I am grateful for their cooperation in letting me use those images—they really help tell the story.

My choice for the subtitle, "America's First City," is not a new concept but one that has come in and out of favor over the years. I have always used that term when talking about Cahokia because of the scale of the site in comparison to other major Mississippian centers—it is many times larger and had more mounds and more people. Some of my colleagues are uncomfortable with the term "city" as it implies the city-state level of sociopolitical organization, although they will accept the term "urbanism" in discussions of Cahokia. There are many different definitions of "city" that can apply to the Cahokia phenomenon. Obviously, it was something more than just a bigger "town," and it had reached a level of complexity not really seen at contemporary sites. Some researchers even suggest that it did reach the level of a city-state.

Michael Smith gives an apt description of what he calls "functional cities," focusing on their role within a regional context:

> An urban settlement is one that is the setting for institutions or activities that are important for a larger hinterland. In this view, one must look beyond the settlement itself and assess its role in the larger society to decide whether it is an urban settlement. There are a variety of urban functions that cities can perform, including political functions (such as the location of the palace or set of political administration), economic functions (the location of craft workshops, markets, warehouses, or other economic institutions), religious functions (a setting for major temples or a pilgrimage center), and cultural functions (a center for artistic production, education, or recreation).

Smith also notes that ancient cities grew through migration from the countryside but also maintained a close interaction between city and countryside. Often there would be many ethnic groups, sometimes organized into neighborhoods. Much of this would seem appropriate in a description of Cahokia and its relationships with outlying communities, as it grew exponentially around AD 1050. Many of the outlying communities were emptied as people migrated to become part of the Cahokia phenomenon, but certain sites were maintained as special-function communities. Also, certain types of ceramics emanating from Arkansas and Missouri are found at Cahokia, suggesting that there were also some long-distance immigrants. It may even be that some of these people brought new ideas and beliefs, contributing to Cahokia's emergence as a city.

Today, there is more of a trend to redefine what constitutes a city, especially one that may not be a city-state. As John Kelly and Jim Brown state in their 2009 paper:

> *We have moved away from traditional models for the Ancient Americas and have focused on the role of religion, ritual, cosmology, and ideology as important elements in the creation and configuration of any single community and how it articulates with smaller communities within the region. We argue here that with respect to site plan, scale, monumentality, and socially differentiated hinterland, Cahokia merits recognition as urban.*

Before Cahokia

About one thousand years ago, a phenomenon occurred in a fertile tract of the Mississippi River flood plain known today as the "American Bottom." This phenomenon came to be called Cahokia Mounds—America's first city. However, Cahokia did not develop in a vacuum. To better understand Cahokia's origins, one must go back in time and space to examine the ancestry of American Indians in North America in order to see what led up to the development of what some scholars have referred to as an Indian "metropolis."

Archaeologists classify Indian cultures in the Americas into two primary periods called the prehistoric and the historic, the former generally referring to the time before the coming of European explorers and settlers and the latter post-dating that incursion. "Prehistoric" commonly is used for cultures with no writing system. This is not to imply that they did not have histories, just that they did not have a system of recording them. All societies have oral traditions that carry on for generations and document their history. In the Americas, only a few of the Mesoamerican cultures—such as the Maya—had a glyphic form of writing.

Thus, the beginning of the historic period will vary from region to region. For instance, in Florida it begins in the mid-1500s with the Spanish occupation and exploration, whereas in Illinois it begins in 1673 with the voyage of Marquette and Joliet; the journals of these expeditions were the first recorded documentation of the peoples they encountered.

THE SETTING

Developments in the American Bottom region and nearby bluffs leading up to the time of Cahokia are representative of regional prehistoric developments and settlements. The American Bottom refers to the region settled in the eighteenth and nineteenth centuries by Americans, who generally displaced the French, English, Spanish and Indians who had preceded them. It is usually considered to be the broad expanse of flood plain on the Illinois side of the Mississippi River opposite St. Louis, Missouri, bounded on the east by the bluffs stretching from Alton on the north to just south of the mouth of the Kaskaskia River near Chester, about eighty miles (128 kilometers) in length. The northern portion of the American Bottom, from Alton to Dupo, Illinois, is the broadest, reaching a maximum east–west width of about eleven miles (18 kilometers) from East St. Louis to Collinsville, Illinois. This "Northern Bottom Expanse" is primarily the result of the confluence of the Missouri and Mississippi Rivers, just south of Alton, especially the scouring action of the meltwaters that flooded these river basins at the end of the last ice age. Later, as the river valley filled with deposits of silt, sand and clay, the river took a meandering course, changing its route many times and swinging from east to west across the valley. As former meanders were cut off from the main channel, they became lakes, sloughs and marshes, which are still evident throughout the American Bottom. A number of creeks draining the eastern uplands captured other old meanders on their way to the Mississippi. The ridge and swale topography of the American Bottom is a result of these meandering river courses, created by the natural levees along the banks and the depressions of the old channels. Settlements were often located on these ridges or on the nearby terraces.

These various stream and lake features formed an interconnected "inland waterway" beyond the eastern banks of the Mississippi. They also provided a superb resource base of fish, waterfowl and aquatic plants. Periodic flooding of the region deposited fertile soils across the terrain of the American Bottom that were important not only to natural flora but also to the eventual use of this area for intensive agriculture. Additionally, the Mississippi Valley is a major flyway for migrating ducks, geese, swans and other waterfowl that were attracted to this expansive wetland setting.

There were scattered woodlands concentrated around the aquatic sources consisting primarily of cottonwood, willow, sycamore, maple and hackberry, surrounded by large areas of wetland prairie. Denser hardwood forests, primarily oaks and hickories, were concentrated along the bluff

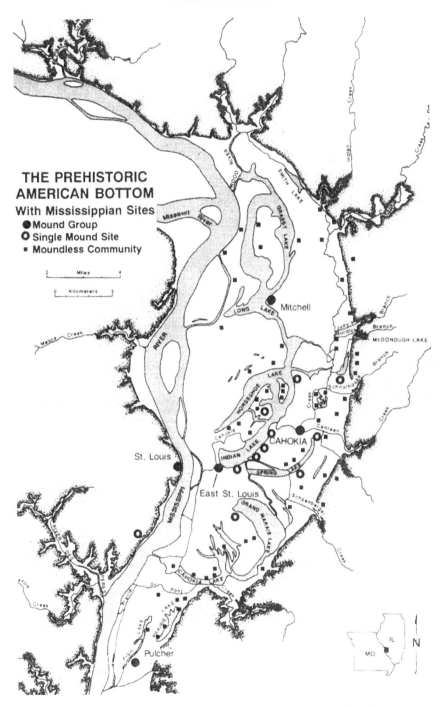

THE PREHISTORIC
AMERICAN BOTTOM
With Mississippian Sites
● Mound Group
○ Single Mound Site
■ Moundless Community

A map of the American Bottom showing rivers, lakes and streams, as well as the locations of Cahokia and other Mississippian towns, villages and farmsteads. *Adapted from map by Mikels Skele.*

slopes and adjacent dissected uplands; bluff crests often were topped with hillside prairies, oaks and cedar; and tallgrass prairies dominated the upland interiors.

These various environmental zones would have provided a stable set of floral and faunal resources within less than a day's walk from any settlement, and ethnobotanical evidence from archaeological sites shows that all zones were being exploited, although to varying degrees in different time periods. However, the stability of these resources would be affected by climatic shifts over many millennia, as well as by increased human exploitation, especially as population densities and distributions increased through time.

CULTURAL TRADITIONS

In eastern North America, four primary prehistoric cultural traditions are recognized by archaeologists: the Paleo-Indian, Archaic, Woodland and Mississippian. Each tradition would be characterized by an assemblage of diagnostic artifact types and forms, settlement patterns, domicile types and environmental utilization. These traditions have early, middle and late phases, and the beginning and ending dates can vary in different geographic zones. There are regional variations, as well as some additional, more localized, traditions.

In the American Bottom region, Paleo-Indian, Archaic, Woodland, Emergent Mississippian, Mississippian and Oneota traditions have been identified. Paleo-Indian is generally believed to have ranged from about 9500 to 8000 BC, although in many parts of the Americas in recent decades a number of sites have been excavated that are pushing back the threshold of the beginning of this period to at least 13,000 BC, if not earlier. The Archaic ranges from 8000 to 600 BC; the Woodland from 600 BC to AD 800; Emergent Mississippian (called Terminal Late Woodland by some archaeologists) from AD 750 to 1050; Mississippian from AD 1050 to 1400; and Oneota from AD 1400 to 1550. Although these dates can vary in different regions, they represent the generally accepted time frames recognized in the American Bottom area. The subphase designations and durations are constantly undergoing revision and refinement as new data accumulates from ongoing research.

TRADITION	PERIOD	CAHOKIA AREA PHASES
PaleoIndian	9500–8000 BC	
Early Archaic	8000–6000 BC	
Middle Archaic	6000–3000 BC	
Late Archaic	**3000–600 BC**	
	3000–2300	Falling Springs
	2300–1900	Titterington
	1900–1450	Mule Road
	1450–1100	Labras Lake
	1100–600	Prairie Lake
Early Woodland	**600–150 BC**	
	600–300	Carr Creek
	500–300	Florence
	300–150	Columbia
Middle Woodland	**150 BC–AD 300**	
	150 BC–50 BC	Cement Hollow
	50 BC–150 AD	Holding
	150–300 AD	Hill Lake
Late Woodland	**AD 300–750**	
	300–450	Rosewood
	450–600	Mund
	600–750	Patrick
Emergent Mississippian/ Terminal Late Woodland	**AD 750–1050**	
	750–800	Sponemann
	800–850	Collinsville
	850–900	Loyd
	900–950	Merrell
	950–1050	Edlehardt
Mississippian	**AD 1050–1400**	
	1050–1100	Lohmann
	1100–1200	Stirling
	1200–1275	Moorehead
	1275–1400	Sand Prairie
Oneota	**AD 1400–1673**	
	1400–1500	Groves
	1500–1673	Vulcan
Historic	**AD 1673–Present**	
	1673–1776	Historic & Colonial Indian
	1776–1820	American Frontier
	1820–1880	Rural & Urban
	1880–1920	Urban & Industrial
	1920–Present	Recent

A time chart of cultural periods and subphases in the Cahokia region.

21

Paleo-Indian

Paleo-Indian peoples first arrived in the American Bottom area around 9500 BC, traveling in small bands. They were relatively nomadic and are sometimes referred to as "big game hunters" as they did occasionally hunt some of the large species of animals that lived in this region at the end of the last ice age, but they also would have hunted smaller animals and gathered some plant foods. There is some debate about what caused the extinction of over thirty species of megafauna, including the mastodon, mammoth, horse, camel, giant sloth, short-faced bear, dire wolf, giant beaver and long-horned bison, many of which were larger than their modern-day cousins. Some say it was the rapidly changing environment following the last ice age, as the climate grew warmer and drier, the ice receded and grasslands and deciduous forests replaced tundra and boreal forest conditions. Favored environmental niches were changing, and the animals would have had difficulty adapting to new ones. However, another factor has also been suggested—the newly introduced Paleo-Indians. They were now hunting these animals, perhaps

Paleo-Indians hunting a mastodon, circa 9000 BC. *Lloyd K. Townsend, Cahokia Mounds State Historic Site.*

killing them faster than they could reproduce. There are even some who suggest diseases may have contributed to the extinctions as other species moved northward following the expansion of the warmer climate into new regions, bringing pathogens to which the megafauna had little or no resistance. Although the majority of experts indicate that the climate change model is the most likely cause, it may well have been a combination of several of the above. One of the best represented sites of this period is at Mastodon State Park, just south of St. Louis near Kimmswick, Missouri. Diagnostic Clovis spear points and other tools were found in association with mastodons and other megafauna.

Clovis points are lanceolate in form with a concave base, and they have a distinctive long flake, or "flute," removed from each side of the base to about one-third to one-half the distance toward the tip. These first appear around 9500 BC, and at some sites in North America archaeologists have discovered "pre-Clovis" levels that date earlier but that have few diagnostic artifacts; however, evidence continues to mount for a pre-Clovis presence.

Archaic

The next period of development is called the Archaic, from 8000 to 600 BC. The climate gradually warmed and was drier for the most part, although there were fluctuations throughout this lengthy time. The glacial masses had retreated, and deciduous forests and grasslands expanded into much of the Midwest, along with a wide range of other flora and fauna. Human populations increased and settlements were at least seasonally occupied. Regional diversity and territorialism became more important. Inhabitants often made use of natural rock shelters where available or built small houses at their base camps or villages. From these they would foray at certain times of the year to establish campsites in order to exploit resources as they became available, such as fishing in the flood plain after the spring floods receded, hunting the migratory waterfowl in the spring and fall and gathering nuts in the uplands in the fall. Fish, mussels and waterfowl were very important in their diet, as were deer, elk, smaller mammals and other birds, and they gathered nuts, berries, roots and other plant resources.

Archaic people began plant husbandry, eventually domesticating varieties of squash, gourds, erect knotweed, marshelder, sunflower and lambsquarter. They also started building a few mounds in some areas, and they made new varieties of "ground stone" tools and ornaments, pecking and grinding

An Archaic family fishing and gathering mussels, nuts and other bottomland resources. *Illinois State Museum diorama.*

granite, basalt, diorite, hematite, banded slate and other varieties of stone, adding to their inventory of chipped chert (flint) tools and weapons. The atlatl, or spear thrower, was the primary weapon, as the bow and arrow would not appear for thousands of years, and their spear points were generally large and well chipped, with a wide variety of stemmed and notched forms that are distinctive for the subphases of Early, Middle and Late Archaic.

In the American Bottom region, the first significant occupations were during the Late Archaic, initially as small base camps and later as extensive occupations of hunting and gathering groups. The fairly permanent settlements were on the higher, more stable, clay meander banks and talus slopes.

Woodland

Following the Archaic was the Woodland tradition. In the American Bottom region, the Early Woodland begins around 600 BC, marked by the introduction of pottery making. Pottery first appears in North America in the Florida area before 2000 BC, but for some reason it did not make it into this region until many centuries later. Woodland pottery also changed through time. The Early Woodland vessels were fairly thick and tempered with grit (crushed rock), and they often had cord-marked bodies and some decorations around the lips and shoulders. Middle Woodland pottery had more variety in shape and decoration, including bowls and jars—some with cord-marked bodies, others with smooth surfaces—and most had some form of neck and rim decoration. Some had more elaborate design work, including stylized birds, geometric patterns and crosshatching around the rim. These are often found in ritual contexts.

There was an increased emphasis on building mounds, mostly conical in form, primarily for mortuary purposes. During Middle Woodland times (300 BC–AD 150), also referred to as "Hopewell," these mounds often had a central log-lined tomb for high-status burials, which were usually accompanied by a wide range of exotic and prestige goods, as well as tools and weapons. Late Woodland (AD 300–750) also has mound burials, but they seldom exhibit the elaborate mortuary practices of the Middle Woodland, and this tradition seems less complex in other ways as well. The pottery is mostly cord-marked to the rim, and occasionally there are decorative lugs on the rim or other types of decoration. However, there were major developments that were notable during Late Woodland.

A Middle Woodland village. *Illinois State Museum diorama.*

The introduction of the bow and arrow sometime around AD 400 greatly changed the hunting strategies as this powerful new weapon allowed harvesting game from greater distances with more accuracy. The primary clue for the newly introduced bow was that suddenly the arrow points were small and lightweight, from one-half inch to one and one-half inches long, often with short stems or having a triangular shape. The smaller lightweight points, compared to the larger Archaic spear points, were necessary for distance and accuracy. These are often mistakenly called "bird points" by collectors, but they were used for all animals of every size and had great penetrating power when propelled by a strong bow.

Agriculture intensified and expanded to include more seed-bearing crops, such as maygrass and little barley, as well as tobacco. Although there is scattered evidence for corn, or maize, during Middle Woodland times, it wasn't until Late Woodland times, after AD 700–800, that it became an important food crop. The widespread cultivation of maize helped foster larger population concentrations, the production of larger food surpluses and the resulting development of more complex political and social organization.

Emergent Mississippian

The transition from the Late Woodland to the Mississippian period begins after AD 750 and is known as Emergent Mississippian, although some archaeologists argue for the term "Terminal Late Woodland." The community pattern usually included organized groupings of houses and other structures arranged around a courtyard, often with a central post that was sometimes surrounded by four pits, and larger structures, probably communal or ceremonial, to one side or in the courtyard area. These formal arrangements suggest the emergence of a ranked form of sociopolitical organization in the American Bottom region and perhaps the appearance of chiefs. The presence of large communities suggests population increases. Their single-family houses are often called "pit houses," as the floors were up to three feet below the surface, with individual postholes for each wall post. Numerous Emergent Mississippian structures and features have been found at the Cahokia site, including some around the typical courtyard arrangement.

Corn had become an even more important crop, providing the quantities and surpluses needed to feed larger populations, but the oily and starchy

An Emergent Mississippian pit house at Cahokia Tract 15-A. *Illinois State Museum.*

seed crops discussed earlier, and many wild plant and animal foods, still contributed in major ways to the diet. With this stable food base a foundation was laid, upon which the massive community of Cahokia could be built.

Mississippian

The Mississippian tradition was forming by AD 1000–1050 but literally expands across the landscape in 1050. Again, we see larger populations and communities, supported by the expanded agricultural complex. As population numbers and densities increased, societal ordering became more complex and formal chiefdoms were established. More well-defined social classes and hierarchies developed; there was increased craft specialization

A Mississippian farming scene. *Vikki Kessler, Cahokia Mounds State Historic Site.*

and division of labor; political alliances became more important; trade was highly structured; and conflicts, and even warfare, between groups and polities increased, perhaps fueled by competition for resources or territory.

Elaborate ritualism also became increasingly important. Perhaps a prime expression of this at Cahokia was the mortuary complex at Mound 72, with an elite burial surrounded by several retainers and exotic grave goods and several associated mass burials, mostly of young women, that suggest human sacrifice. Also, construction of a Woodhenge, a circular arrangement of large cedar posts with a central observation post, is another indicator of some of the ritual activities and structures. From the center post, the sun priest could observe the rising sun on the eastern horizon as it lined up with certain perimeter posts. This calendar could be used to determine the winter and summer solstices and spring and fall equinoxes, as well as other important dates in the ceremonial cycle. There were at least five Woodhenges built at Cahokia in the same general location.

During Mississippian, new ceramic forms appeared with a greater variety of form and style than previously seen, and gradually the majority of wares was tempered with burned and crushed mussel shell, mixed with a paste made from local clay outcrops. There was an increase in exotic wares from distant regions, primarily from the South, most likely used as containers for commodities being traded rather than the pottery itself being traded.

Clockwise from top, left:
A cylindrical black beaker, burnished, with an excised scroll design similar to southeastern styles. *Cahokia Mounds State Historic Site.*
A beaver effigy bowl. *Illinois State Museum.*
A Powell Plain jar with a burnished surface. *Cahokia Mounds State Historic Site.*
A storage jar with a Ramey Incised design on the shoulder. *Cahokia Mounds State Historic Site.*

A Mississippian temple mound. *Illinois State Museum diorama.*

Cahokia ceramics, or copies of them, appear in many areas of the Midwest and Southeast. Exchange networks were well developed and growing, probably under the control of high-ranking personages.

Settlement patterns also changed, and there was greater variety in community size. During most of the Mississippian phases, communities outside of Cahokia were small and moundless, referred to as homesteads, farmsteads or hamlets. However, a number of villages of small to moderate size were scattered throughout the area, some with one or two mounds, which were probably local centers with special functions. The mounds were primarily rectangular platforms that elevated important buildings.

There was eventually a nucleation of settlement associated with the Cahokia site and some smaller administrative centers, or satellite communities, mostly identifiable as multiple-mound towns, or "temple towns," such as those in the present-day communities of St. Louis, Missouri, and East St. Louis, Dupo and Mitchell, Illinois. Some of these grew contemporary with Cahokia, but not all survived as long, nor were their peak periods of equal duration.

In this immediate area we had three of the largest communities in the Mississippian world—Cahokia with 120 mounds, East St. Louis with

45 mounds and St. Louis with 26 mounds (it used to have the nickname "Mound City"). Unfortunately, the latter two sites fell prey to urban expansion and were essentially destroyed by 1870. At their inception, some of these communities may have been equal in power or size to Cahokia, but Cahokia soon outpaced them and dominated the area for at least a couple of centuries. Cahokia had sudden growth in what has been called the "Big Bang" during the Lohmann phase (AD 1050–1100), but the subsequent Stirling phase (AD 1100–1200) was also a time of dense population and elaborate cultural complexity, and Cahokia rose to dominance as the largest prehistoric settlement in America.

A City of Mounds

MOUNDS

Cahokia has the largest concentration of mounds for a Mississippian site. Approximately 109 have been documented, but the total was probably about 120 across an area of nearly six square miles. About 80 remain in some form, and the locations of 72 whole or partial mounds are now protected as part of the 2,200-acre Cahokia Mounds State Historic Site. The majority of these have had some modern impact—plowed over, sold for fill or partially destroyed by construction. Others even had houses, a discount store or a trailer park built on top of them. Only a few have escaped somewhat intact. In fact, it is difficult to determine the original shape of many of the mounds, especially the smaller ones that were plowed over for so many years before the state acquired them. Fortunately, some of the early maps from the late 1800s often give information on shape, size and height, and some new technology involving micro-mapping and analysis of slopewash soils around the bases of the mounds can help determine original forms.

The majority of the mounds were rectangular and flat topped, often called "temple mounds," or "platform mounds," as it is believed that they supported religious or ceremonial structures, governmental buildings or council lodges and the homes of some of the elite. They vary greatly in size, from a few feet tall to the massive one-hundred-foot-high Monks Mound. Some platform mounds have additional terraces or extensions,

A City of Mounds

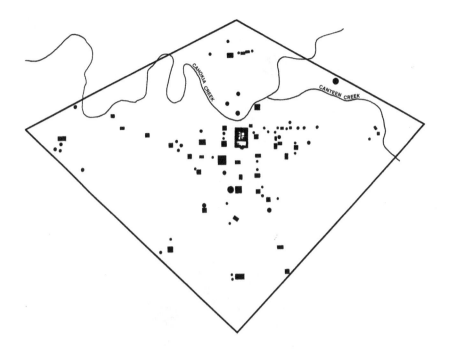

A map of the distribution of mounds at Cahokia over a six-square-mile area. *Cahokia Mounds State Historic Site.*

and Monks Mound has three or four terraces, depending on how one interprets the "Second Terrace," which is discussed in more detail in the Monks Mound chapter.

The other types of mounds at Cahokia were conical and ridgetop in form, the latter being unique to the Cahokia area. These forms are believed to have marked important locations and also served mortuary and other ceremonial functions.

Conical forms were common as burial mounds during the preceding Woodland period, and this function continued somewhat into the Mississippian. However, at Cahokia, there has not been a thorough excavation of a conical mound to confirm whether it served burial functions or some other purpose. At some other Mississippian sites, burials have been found associated with some conical mounds. It is also possible that some of those noted as conical may have had a circular base and a circular platform summit, perhaps even with a structure, rather than true conical forms.

Some conicals are paired with platform mounds at Cahokia, and it is believed that they may have had a mortuary function. Two notable examples

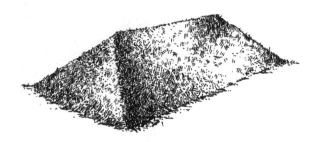

RIDGETOP

CONICAL

PLATFORM

The three mound types found at Cahokia. Ridgetop mounds are unique to the Cahokia area. *Al Meyer, Cahokia Mounds State Historic Site.*

are the Twin Mounds and the Little Twin Mounds. The Twin Mounds, forty-five feet tall, sit at the south end of the Grand Plaza opposite Monks Mound, and the Little Twin Mounds are southwest of the Twin Mounds, just west of the largest borrow pit at the site. Testing around both of these mound pairs showed that each set was built on a low platform that connected them, and the Little Twin Mounds had a low causeway or ridge connecting them. Some researchers believe that a charnel structure, where bodies of the elite were prepared for burial or stored, would have been located on the platform mound, and the bodies might have been later buried in the conical mound. However, neither of these paired mound complexes has been excavated to confirm this function.

The third type of mound at Cahokia is the ridgetop mound, longer than it is wide and coming to a crest at the top, roof-like in appearance. These also vary greatly in size, from 6 feet tall and 140 feet long (Mound 72) to as much as 25 feet tall and 433 feet long (Rattlesnake/Harding Mound—No. 66) and 40 feet tall and 300 feet long (Powell Mound—No. 86). There are at least six ridgetop mounds at Cahokia and possibly a couple more (but their original shapes are difficult to determine due to plowing). Most of them appear to be oriented along the major north–south and east–west axes of the site, and the largest ones (Powell and Rattlesnake) are at the western and southern limits of the site. Thus, these mounds have often been referred to as "marker mounds," but they probably had several functions. When excavations occurred in Rattlesnake Mound, Powell Mound and Mound 72, burials were encountered, some in mass graves, confirming that at least some ridgetop mounds had associated mortuary functions. Powell, Mound 72 and Mound 49 also showed that earlier platform mounds were covered by a final capping of soil to form the ridgetop shape, perhaps in a ritual of closure.

The largest concentration of mounds is around the center of the site, dominated by Monks Mound. However, there are clusters of mounds at the extreme limits of the site, such as the Kunnemann Group to the north, the Rattlesnake Group to the south, the Powell Group to the west and the Rouch Group to the southwest. The East Group does have a number of mounds, but many of them, other than Mound 1 and Mound 2, do not show up on most of the early maps of Cahokia and first appear on a 1935 U.S. Geological Survey (USGS) map of the region. It is now known that in the 1930s a small golf course was built at that part of the site, and some of these mounds (Nos. 97–104) may have been formed during the construction of the golf course, perhaps as tees or greens. Most have been lost to construction. Test excavations in Mound 1, the easternmost mound in the Cahokia group, show that it was indeed a mound but had additional soil added to it historically, and at least two houses were built sequentially there in the twentieth century. Mound 2, adjacent to it, also had a house on it, obscuring its form, but it may have been a ridgetop mound originally.

At the western end of the site was the Powell Mound, which unfortunately was destroyed in the winter of 1930–31. A ridgetop, it was one of the largest mounds at Cahokia. However, it was originally a platform mound about half as tall. This was exposed when a steam shovel hired by the farmer/owner removed the mound to fill a low area nearby to increase his tillable land. Ironically, this may have been the borrow pit from which soil had been removed to build the mound. (See "Other Plazas, Mounds and Structures.")

We know relatively little about the dates for most of the mounds. Although there has been some type of testing (partial excavation, test units, coring and augering) with almost fifty of the mounds, many of those tests were done early in Cahokia research, before carbon dating, or did not produce datable materials. What has been noted, however, is that most mounds had several stages of construction. How much time passed between the stages is not clear, nor is the reason for the enlargements. Some possible reasons would include periodic episodes of ritual renewal based on some calendar cycle; the death of a leader or other important personage; perhaps individual kin or social groups that maintained certain mounds had rituals that required enlarging or capping mounds; or perhaps as mounds were exposed to the elements and suffered from erosion, they were regularly repaired and renewed. Soil core tests, such as in the large Mound 48, suggest that some mounds may have been built in one episode, as indicated by the homogeneous fill, but most excavations into them indicate at least a couple of stages.

When mounds are excavated, it is clear that the soils often came from several sources of different color and texture—clay, silt and sandy soils or mixtures of these. Most of this was extracted from nearby borrow pits and probably from the nearby creek bottoms. The soil was dug with stone hoes and wooden and shell tools and carried in baskets or bags to the construction site, where it was deposited, sometimes in piles and other times spread out in thin layers. In the excavations, one can often see the actual basket loads as lenses of different colored soils, and it is estimated that an average load would have been between forty and sixty pounds, or a little over one cubic foot. Most likely, it was compacted by stomping with the feet or using tamping poles. In some areas, "sod blocks" had been cut from the ground surface and stacked upside down as a construction technique. Some recent repair work on Monks Mound revealed that all three techniques were utilized.

A City of Mounds

Powell Mound being steam shoveled away in 1931. Note the dark line in the profile showing a former flat-topped surface before it was made into a ridgetop mound. *Illinois State Museum.*

Excavating soil and carrying it in baskets to the mound construction site. *Cahokia Mounds State Historic Site.*

In most cases where there have been mound excavations at Cahokia, there is evidence that before a mound was built the surface area was stripped, perhaps to level it. It is likely that much of this soil was then used in mound construction. Sometimes a thin layer of special soil, such as light-colored sand, was laid down initially, undoubtedly in some symbolic ritual. Soil types and colors are known to have been important to later Indian groups, and this also would have been true for prehistoric Indians. At the Shiloh Mounds in Tennessee, red and yellow soils were used to surface a mound. Mound 55 and several others at Cahokia appear to have at least one stage covered with black clay, and a recent exposure of part of the east side of Monks Mound suggests that a light-colored soil covered a former slope surface.

Most artists' illustrations of Cahokia show grass-covered mounds. It is possible that mounds no longer in use had vegetation on them, but while in use they probably had relatively bare surfaces. Currently, there is much discussion about this among archaeologists, with perhaps the majority now favoring the bare-surface concept. This would have entailed a lot of maintenance to keep the surface free of weeds and scrub vegetation and would have required repeated repairs after exposure to the forces of weather. In fact, this has been seen in some of the work on Monks Mound—erosional gullies that probably washed out in thunderstorms clearly had been filled in a series of repair episodes. Perhaps there was a segment of the population that was responsible for upkeep and repairs to mounds. Excavations at the base of Monks Mound on both the east and west sides revealed numerous thin layers of slopewash that probably were deposited during storms when the mound was under a period of construction and before the surface had been stabilized. Today, vegetation covers all of the mounds and helps to stem surface erosion. However, slumping, which is a much deeper problem, has occurred both in prehistoric and recent times on Monks Mound as a result of the buildup of internal water, which weakens the internal structure. The sides eventually give way, and sections flow downward as a large mass slides along a deep crack.

BORROW PITS

A number of borrow pits, where soil was extracted for construction of mounds, are still evident around the Cahokia site as shallow to deep depressions in the terrain. The majority are in the southern half of the site, which tends to have more clay and silty clay soils, often underlain by sandy deposits. All of these soils were deposited by the meanderings of the Mississippi River across the American Bottom over many millennia, and examples of all of them have been observed in mound construction. Some borrowing appears to have been done in former habitation areas, as there is often village refuse included in some mound fill. It appears that besides digging borrow pits to extract these soils, the Cahokians were also utilizing soils from the Cahokia Creek bottom, which runs through the site. The absence of village debris in some mound fills and the types of soils used, especially those observed in parts of Monks Mound, support this hypothesis.

Most of the borrow pits have silted in over the years as a result of natural processes and modern cultivation of the surrounding areas. Some testing in Cahokia's largest borrow pit, south of the Twin Mounds, revealed several feet of deposits, and this is undoubtedly true of most of the other pits as well. During rainy seasons, these pits often fill with water for long periods of time. During Mississippian times as well, these borrow pits probably held water, which would have been stagnant and not potable—the running water of Cahokia and Canteen Creeks would have been the primary sources for water for cooking and drinking.

Several former borrow pits were ultimately filled in with community refuse, such as the one beneath Mound 51, just southeast of Monks Mound. Perhaps some of the soil used to build Monks Mound or the Grand Plaza came from there. The archaeological excavations in this borrow pit suggest that much of the debris probably came from feasting and ceremonies that took place in the Grand Plaza at the center of the site. (See "The Grand Plaza and Its Mounds.")

Another smaller borrow pit was detected by remote sensing in the Grand Plaza, just southwest of Mound 56, and may have been the source for soils used to build that mound. Subsequent excavations revealed that it had been refilled in a fairly rapid manner, perhaps as the Grand Plaza was being expanded and leveled. It is unknown at this time how many other possible borrow pits or borrow areas there are at Cahokia that are no longer visible. Testing west of the base of Monks Mound indicates that there was much borrowing there, and another borrow area was identified north of Mound 34. There are also several borrow areas east of the Grand Plaza and its surrounding mounds. It is not known how many other buried borrow pits or areas may have been filled in and covered over as the city plan changed.

"Stupendous" Monks Mound

D ominating the center of Cahokia is Monks Mound, referred to in 1811 by Henry Brackenridge, in the first written documentation of the site, as a "stupendous pile of earth." Indeed, it is stupendous in many ways. It is the tallest mound, covers the most area and contains the most volume of any prehistoric earthen monument in the Americas. Descriptions of its dimensions have varied quite a bit over the years, as some were "guestimates" as to its height, length and width, while others were based on either simple or more precise surveying techniques.

The mound is basically rectangular in form, with its north–south alignment oriented about six degrees east of north. Today it has four terraces, the most of any Mississippian mound, each with its own characteristics and history. The First Terrace is the largest, and it extends across the full south side of the mound at a height of about nine meters (thirty feet). It has a ramp that extends over eighteen meters (sixty feet) to the south. The west end is slightly higher due to the fact that there was a small mound on that corner that had several stages of construction.

The Second Terrace on the west side is an irregular series of ridges and gullies, with one area toward the southern end that was relatively flat and about twenty-one meters (seventy feet) high. As will be discussed later, it is possible that the Second Terrace was once part of the summit of the mound and collapsed at some point, but I will continue to use this term since there is an elevation, however irregular, existing today on the west side that historically has been called the Second Terrace.

An aerial view of the one-hundred-foot-high Monks Mound, the largest prehistoric earthwork in the Americas. *Cahokia Mounds State Historic Site.*

The Third Terrace is the south half of the summit, at a height of about twenty-nine meters (ninety-five feet), and it covers less than a half acre. Amos Hill built a house and several outbuildings on this terrace in 1830 and cut a trail up the west side to access his complex. He also dug a well nearly twenty-seven meters (ninety feet) deep on the Second Terrace, lined with limestone cobbles. There was a smaller conical mound somewhere on the Third Terrace that Hill leveled when he built his farm complex, and it may have been on the southeast corner, or at least pushed over in that direction, as there is a bulge in the mound at that corner.

The Fourth Terrace covers the north half of the summit at about 30.5 meters (one hundred feet) high, and it covers nearly one acre (0.4 hectares). Excavations, which will be discussed later, revealed that a huge structure once stood at that end of the mound, possibly before the final capping of the Fourth Terrace, and it is believed that from there, the paramount chief would have ruled Cahokia and the surrounding region.

The 100-foot height of Monks Mound has been established by mapping of the mound by various professional survey teams over the years and through vertical coring of the mound done in the 1960s. There are fluctuations in

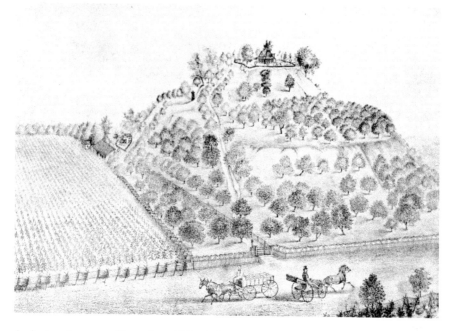

A nineteenth-century illustration of Monks Mound with the home of T.T. Ramey on top (originally built by Amos Hill), the well on the Second Terrace and the small Ramey house and barn at back. In the foreground is Collinsville Road, part of the National Road. *1873 Madison County Atlas.*

the surface elevation of the Fourth Terrace due to settling and erosion, but most readings are within a few feet (plus or minus) of the 100-foot figure. To get the best determination of the height (other than coring), one needs to get beyond the slopewash into the surrounding terrain, where the average elevation is 128 meters (420 feet) above sea level. The elevation of the highest point on the mound is 158 meters (520 feet).

Its basal dimensions are a little more difficult to ascertain, as there has been extensive slumping and slopewash over the centuries that make its sides irregular, especially on the west, north and east sides, and estimates range from 5.7 to 6.9 hectares (fourteen to seventeen acres), depending on which elevation contour is used. Today, its general dimensions range about 317 meters (1,040 feet) by 241 meters (790 feet); however, if one assumes that the original mound form was more regularly rectangular and draws straight lines through all of the undulations and irregularities, the north–south length approximates 277 meters (910 feet), including the 20 meters (65 feet) of the south ramp. The east–west width is about 219 meters (720 feet). This gives an area of about fourteen acres (5.7 hectares), which is greater than

A one-foot-interval contour map of Monks Mound, 2007. *Cahokia Mounds State Historic Site.*

the base area of the Great Pyramid of Cheops in Egypt and the Pyramid of the Sun at Teotihuacan, Mexico, both of which are about thirteen acres. However, both of those structures are much taller. In the Americas, Monks Mound comes in third in total size of all the pyramids, superseded by the largest Mexican pyramid at Cholula, Mexico, and the Pyramid of the Sun at Teotihuacan.

The volume of Monks Mound has been estimated at nearly 623,000 cubic meters (22 million cubic feet), although Tim Schilling of Washington University recently estimated the volume as high as 740,000 cubic meters (over 26 million cubic feet). All of this soil was dug and carried by hand in baskets and bags. Much of the soil probably was excavated from the nearby Cahokia Creek bottom, as well as from a variety of borrow pits throughout the site. There is quite a mixture of soils in the fill, from sands and silts to clays and loams, and they all appear to be local soils from the surrounding flood plain and old river and creek bottoms.

It has been suggested by William Woods that in some parts of the mound the use of alternating layers of coarse- and fine-grained soils might have been engineered to facilitate drainage and provide stability, but this has been questioned to some degree by other archaeologists, who suggest that the alternating layers are not consistent over large areas; instead, they may represent differential loading and spreading of soils from several sources or layers within a borrow area, and the layering effect may be circumstantial. It is possible that at different stages of construction or in certain parts of the mound, different strategies of construction were used. Indeed, when a portion of the east side of the mound was exposed during slump repairs in 2007, at least three techniques were observed: clumps of basket-loaded soils, bands of thinner layering or strewn soils and inverted sod blocks. Additionally, there were several areas where erosional gullies in the surface had been repaired by filling them with basket loads of mixed soils.

Although, as stated earlier, most artists' renderings of Monks Mound show it covered with green vegetation, it has been suggested by Timothy Pauketat that Monks Mound was covered in a layer of black clay. This is somewhat based on a horizontal layer of dark clay exposed in the 2007 repair project on the east side of the mound and Nelson Reed's recent publication on his excavations on top of the mound. However, on the downslope of the exposed slump profile, it seems that a light-colored layer of silty soil once covered a former surface of the slope. It is known that at the Mississippian Shiloh Mound site in Tennessee, colored soils—especially red and yellow—were selected for covering that mound. Also, Harriet Smith's 1941 excavations of Mound 55, the Murdock Mound, at Cahokia revealed a black clay surface on one of the construction stages. Colors had meaning to Indian societies, and it is possible that the mound was surfaced with colored soil to represent certain beliefs or cosmology, but more testing would be needed to see if the colors are consistently applied to Monks Mound and whether it was a dark or light soil or some other type. Some soils were probably selected for their plasticity, ability to hold up to weather when wet or dry, strength in holding against erosion or some other purpose, and the color choices may just be circumstantial.

If there was vegetation, such as short prairie grasses, on the sides of the mound to help protect against erosion, it apparently did not grow enough over time to establish a visible humus layer before another mound stage was added. On the summit, one would expect sandy soils to be used to provide secure footing, especially in wet weather, similar to the sandy layer on the Grand Plaza.

PRESERVING MONKS MOUND

The first relatively accurate map of Monks Mound was made in the 1870s, commissioned by Dr. J.J.R. Patrick, a Belleville dentist and antiquarian. It was part of a project to map the whole site that documented the shapes and sizes of most of the mounds. In the late 1800s, there were a number of other maps made of the site, including representations of Monks Mound, but many were schematic, not as accurate as the Patrick map and sometimes copied from one another. Patrick also produced cast-iron models of Monks Mound, one as it appeared in the 1870s and another a projection of what the original appearance may have been. This model gives a good reference for seeing how the mound has changed in the last 140 years. The most notable changes are on the west and north sides.

Before excavations and other testing took place, there was some debate about whether Monks Mound and the other mounds were Indian-made or natural, with perhaps some alteration by the Indians. About 1914, Dr. A.R. Crook, a geologist and director of the Illinois State Museum, did the first official testing of Monks Mound by putting twenty-five auger holes into its north face. He did not believe that the mounds were man-made and, like some other geologists, thought that they were erosional remnants left by the meandering of the Mississippi or the movement of glaciers during the last ice age, or some combination of the two.

In the early 1920s, the first "professional" but not formally trained archaeologist, Warren K. Moorehead, visited the site and made arrangements to conduct excavations to prove that these were man-made and not natural formations. He had dug at a number of other mound sites and knew that they were of Indian construction; he wanted to prove the same at Cahokia.

With geologist Morris Leighton, he began testing the mounds in 1922, including several test pits on the Fourth Terrace and on the east side of Monks Mound, which he then augered to a total depth of about twenty feet. These tests showed that the mound was not a natural feature but man-made. Crook then somewhat regrettably changed his opinion, admitting that the evidence was convincing.

Since the turn of the century, there had been many attempts by a number of groups and legislators at passing legislation to create a park, either state or national, all of which had failed for various reasons, including the suspicion that the mounds were natural. But with Moorehead's work on many mounds and village areas proving that this was once a significant prehistoric community, and his taking the legislature to task in many newspapers, the state eventually acquired the original 144.4 acres (fifty-eight hectares) from the Ramey family (unfortunately through eminent domain), including Monks Mound, and Cahokia Mounds State Park was created in 1925.

EXCAVATIONS AND RESEARCH ON THE SUMMIT

No further work on Monks Mound is documented until 1964, when Washington University began work on the Fourth Terrace, coordinated by Nelson Reed, with James Porter and Chuck Bareis directing the excavations of a number of test units, including one at the interface with the Third Terrace that revealed remnants of the farm structure belonging to Amos Hill and, later, the Ramey family. Several small wall trenches were identified, as was a large post pit in the middle of the terrace. In 1965, the work was greatly expanded, with Reed and J.W. Bennett coordinating and Porter directing the fieldwork. Seven deep vertical cores were drilled through the mound across the Fourth and Third Terraces, and a couple more on the First and Second Terraces, to determine information about its internal structure and possible building stages. One excavation unit was over five meters deep and was placed to cross-section the upper portion of one of the core holes. That way they could compare what they were seeing in the cores and what actually existed in the mound fill. They thought that narrow bands of limonite might indicate former surfaces, and based on the continuation of some of these bands across several cores, they suggested anywhere from eight to fourteen building stages between AD 900 and 1150, according to

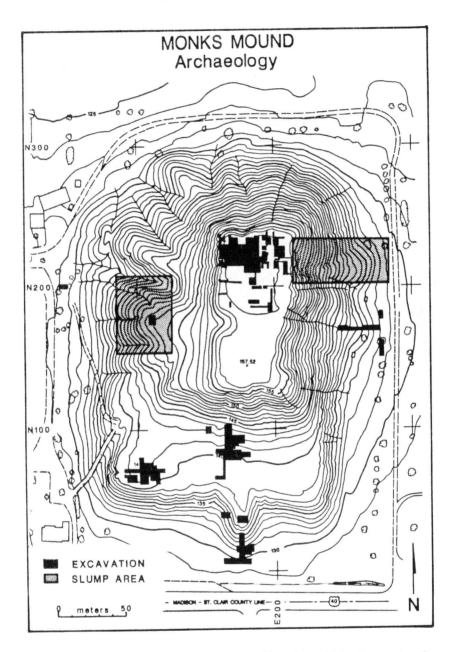

A map of Monks Mound excavations through 1991. Since then, additional excavations for the new stairs have been done on the South Ramp and the slope to the Third Terrace, and repairs have been made to slumps on the east side and northwest corner. *Mikels Skele, Illinois Historic Preservation Agency.*

An aerial view of the 1971 Fourth Terrace excavations by Washington University. *Richard Norrish, Cahokia Mounds State Historic Site.*

radiocarbon dates. However, more recent work on the mound suggests a later beginning date, and Tim Schilling says that construction could have taken place in a shorter span of time, possibly as little as thirty years, but more research is needed to support that concept.

Reed continued work through 1971 on the summit, with Glen Freimuth, Larry Conrad and Fred Fischer directing in various years. Expanded areas were opened at the back of the Fourth Terrace, and large wall trenches were exposed, some forming the outline of a building that was about 31.7 by 14.6 meters (104 by 48 feet) and oriented east to west. It also had several large, deep post pits down the center that would have held the tall roof supports. It was essentially barren of artifacts, indicating that it was ceremonial in nature and had been cleaned out. There is speculation as to its function, including being the residence of the paramount chief, a storage area for the bones of deceased leaders, a council lodge for elders and leaders or some combination thereof. Nonetheless, it was from here that Cahokia would be governed and major rituals would take place. There is some evidence of possible rebuilding of the structure, and there were several small ancillary structures near it, including one with an unusual zigzagging wall trench pattern of unknown function.

HOW THE TEMPLE AND COURTYARD MAY HAVE APPEARED

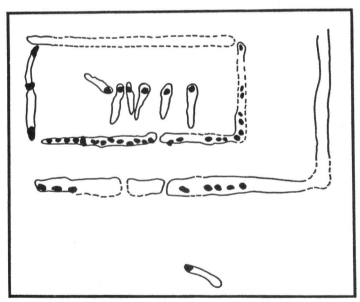

EXCAVATION MAP OF THE LAST TEMPLE ON THE FOURTH TERRACE— WITH COURTYARD, FENCE, AND LARGE POST A.D. 1150

Schematic drawings of the Fourth Terrace and an outline of the trenches and post pits for the large building and the courtyard fence. *Cahokia Mounds State Historic Site.*

Another large wall trench around the building appears to represent a substantial fence, or palisade, creating a courtyard, especially on the east and south sides of the building. However, as seen today, the building abuts the present slopes on the north and west sides. It might be anticipated that the building would have been centered at the back of the mound, with equal space for a courtyard all around it, rather than offset like this. There is some obvious evidence for slumping and erosion on the north side of the mound, which would account for missing portions of the back wall of the building. The west wall trench, when excavated, looked different than the others, almost like it was some type of repair, and it abuts the west slope of the mound, which leads down to the irregular Second Terrace. To dig a trench and have a structure wall that close to the slope would present the danger of it shearing off.

Thus, there is a new interpretation that what we call the Second Terrace was once up at the same height as the summit and that at some point there was a major slump, or collapse, of the west side that may have taken part of the building with it. In fact, when Bill Woods and crew calculated the mass of earth on that side and compared it to the mass represented by the courtyard area east of the building, it was a very similar amount. Whether the collapse was a result of an earthquake episode, as suggested by Woods, or the buildup of internal water in the mound, which continues to be a problem today, is open to interpretation.

When Reed's crews were excavating the summit, they were not able to detect much in the way of features in the top seventy centimeters of soil, and it was not until they were at that depth that most of the features discussed were observed. It would seem that this top layer may have been a final capping of that space upon termination of its use.

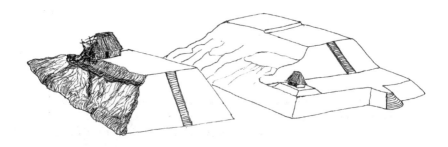

The west side of Monks Mound slumped and may have taken part of the building with it. The First Terrace was added, repairs were made to the west side and the summit was capped and sealed. *William Iseminger.*

Over the past five years, several crews have done remote sensing on the top of Monks Mound, but with limited success. SIUC and Washington University (WU) crews tested on the Third Terrace and could detect what appear to be indications of a cellar or other features associated with the Hill/Ramey farmhouse on that terrace but not much that could be clearly associated with prehistoric activity. The deeper sensing of the WU system revealed what may be some of the trapped water levels inside the mound, or at least some very wet clay zones, mostly under the Third Terrace area.

FIRST TERRACE INVESTIGATIONS

Also starting in 1964 and continuing sporadically through 1972, Chuck Bareis, working with field crews from the University of Illinois, examined the interface between the First Terrace and the slope up to the Third Terrace. His work exposed several interesting features, including what appeared to be a technique used to enlarge the mound. He found that small mounds of mostly clay soils were placed at the base of the slope and that less dense soils were then placed behind them and up the slope. These basal mound ridges then served like buttresses to help support the slope and prevent slumping, and the less dense soils helped provide better drainage. These were then capped with sandy soil in a series of irregular "plateaus," or mini-terraces, which were in turn capped with brown silty clay. Whether these were part of some type of stairway or other architectural feature is unclear.

Bareis also found a series of wall trenches running east to west across the middle of the terrace, their function unknown. He believed that they may have marked a former front of the terrace and that these served as the fences or screens across a former front of the mound that shielded activities there from view by the general public. It was common to have such screens on terrace edges, as has been seen at several other Mississippian mound sites. Bareis was one of the first to suggest that the First Terrace was a late addition to the front of the mound, based on slope angles he saw in his profiles, perhaps to buttress the front from slumping such as may have been occurring on other sides of the mound. He also suggested that, based on the different soils he saw in his profiles, soil engineering was taking place; certain soils were selected for certain tasks.

On the southwest corner of the First Terrace, Elizabeth Benchley conducted excavations for the University of Wisconsin–Milwaukee, working

for Melvin Fowler to examine this area where there was a slight rise. Fowler had suggested there might be another marker post at this location since it occurred along his hypothetical north–south center line for the Cahokia site, and in 1967, he had found a large post where that line intersected Mound 72 (see "The Mysteries of Mound 72"). This was also the top point of an equilateral triangle he had determined, drawing an east–west line between Mound 68 and Mound 62 and extending an equal-length line from each to the north, where they converged on the southwest corner of Monks Mound. Bisecting that triangle resulted in his north–south centerline.

Above: The First Terrace southwest corner UWM excavations showing burned structures covered by several stages of small mound construction. *Cahokia Mounds State Historic Site.*

Opposite: An aerial view showing the Monks Mound First Terrace excavation (U of I) and the trench in front of the South Ramp (WU), 1971. *Cahokia Mounds State Historic Site.*

Benchley's excavations took place in 1967–68 and 1971, and she found that this was an area of intensive activity and construction. Initially, there had been at least two large buildings and possibly a couple more, arranged around a courtyard that centered on the location where Fowler thought there might be a post. No post was found at that position, although there were some pits. The structures had been burned and the floors baked hard in the process, probably in a ritual of renewal and closure, as this location was next the scene of construction of a small platform mound about 1.0 meter high, with a new building on top and a ramp to the east. Over time, there were nine building stages to this mound, enlarged in small increments to 1.4 meters high. What is curious is that there were superimposed posts on the slopes of several of these mound stages at the location where Fowler was hoping to find a marker post for his centerline. These were nowhere near the size of the post in Mound 72, but their unusual positioning lends some support to his hypothesis—it was almost as if they were carrying on a tradition of having a post at that location and recognizing its significance. To the north of the mound, there was an area of dark fill with late Mississippian debris that formed a wide, ramp-like connection to the base of the Second Terrace. Although some features were present, the purpose of that filled zone is uncertain.

Benchley also found a number of historic Indian burials with French trade goods dating to the mid-1700s, including glass and catlinite beads, a brass bell and one burial that had been in a wooden box with a French lockplate and key. There were also a number of structural artifacts such as nails, shutter hooks and other hardware. When examining the excavation records at a later date, Benchley and John Walthall realized there was a pattern to a number of postholes and the distribution of the historic artifacts. They also found in some old records concerning a cantine, or French trading post, reference to it being near the former location of the chapel on the south face of the "great Nob." They then realized that this historical material was related to that chapel.

Apparently, the Cahokia subtribe of the Illiniwek (Illinois), who had been living in the locale of the French village of Cahokia about ten miles south of the mounds, had been creating problems. The French decided about 1735 to move them away from the village, establishing a settlement for them at Monks Mound, building the chapel and plowing some fields for them. The Cahokia were apparently here until 1752, when conflicts with other Indian tribes led to their demise.

The mounds were once called the "Cantine Mounds" due to the former presence of the cantine, but in the mid-1800s some local historians thought

One of the final stages of the small mound on the southwest corner of the First Terrace. *Cahokia Mounds State Historic Site.*

it would be a good idea to begin calling them "Cahokia Mounds" to honor the presence of the Cahokia, even though they were not responsible for building the mounds. The Cahokia had originally been up around the Great Lakes in Ohio, Indiana and Illinois but were forced west and south by other tribes during the fur trade era in the early 1600s.

Monks Mound apparently was called "Abbe Hill" by some people in the late 1700s, and Cahokia Creek was once called "River L'Abbe" (Priest's River) in reference to a priest who had a mill on the stream and conducted services in the chapel on Monks Mound with other priests from the order of the Seminary of Foreign Missions. It became known locally as Monks Mound from the presence of Trappist monks at the site in the early 1800s; they lived on another mound and gardened the terraces of this mound.

When Bareis was excavating at the center of the First Terrace, he also found some burials with associated historic artifacts, and in the late 1990s, when SIUE was doing excavations for the footings for the permanent stairway up the mound, archaeologists found several pits full of debris, including French period artifacts, as well as horse, bear, swan, gar and an abundance of other animal remains. This suggests that some type of feasting was taking place, and it is likely that the settlement of the Cahokia was here on the First Terrace. Remote sensing at the east end of the First Terrace by John Sexton from SIUC identified disturbances there, but it is not clear what they represent—prehistoric or historic features, or both.

In 1971, Nelson Reed had a WU crew under Ted Lotz conduct test excavations on the South Ramp, which extends southward from the south edge of the First Terrace. The ramp is not at the center of the terrace but is offset to the east, aligning more with the center of the Third Terrace at the summit of the mound. Reed's tests were to examine this architectural feature, which is thought to be the main point of access to Monks Mound from the Grand Plaza. The trench up the ramp revealed that there had been at least three construction stages, each with a different colored soil, which Reed labeled the red, yellow and brown ramps, although the soils were actually subtle shades of those colors. The surface of the yellow ramp had a series of undulations that appear to represent where log steps were once placed and had either been removed or decayed in place. A number of small post molds were also seen, generally conforming to the proposed step locations, which Reed interprets as the locations of pegs used to hold the steps in place. When all of this was mapped, it appeared that the step configuration was curving around the front of the ramp, which would be unique. At the top of the ramp, there were several post molds that he believes represent a possible gate or entrance to the First Terrace and that were likely part of a fence or screen that ran along the edges of the terrace.

SECOND TERRACE TESTING

In 1985, a slumping event occurred on the Second Terrace, when one section dropped three to four feet. Bill Woods and Jim Collins, along with several helpers from SIUE, made profiles at several locations along the slump scarp and put a 6.00- by 4.00-meter test unit into a relatively level part of the terrace. Little was found in the upper zone of the unit, as it was mostly slopewash deposits from farther up the mound. In the middle zone, there was an irregular shallow basin feature of unknown function. The lower zone exhibited basket loading of mixed soils and a large post pit about 1.00 meter in diameter and 1.75 meters (5.7 feet) deep. The question arises as to whether the features encountered here were preexisting when the Second Terrace was at the level of the summit and maintained their integrity as the west side of the mound slumped, or if they were emplaced after the slumping and the Second Terrace was modified and used at its new and lower elevation. The initial interpretation was that it was built as a specific terrace, but now the additional data suggests that it is part of the collapsed summit of the mound. Woods also suggests that the moist clay core of the mound dried out and cracked when local industries pumped out and lowered the regional water table and that later, as those industries failed or left the area, the water table rose again, remoistening the core. However, the core was now fragmented and not as stable as it once had been, leading to its failure. All of these factors may be involved, and some people have suggested that vibrations from nearby Interstate 55/70 may have contributed or that cutting the trees off the mound in the mid-1960s was a cause. However, all of the engineers we have talked with say that tree cutting would not be a factor because the slip faces of the slump go much deeper than the roots of the trees. In fact, the trees caused harm to the mound as their roots disturbed the archaeology, especially when a tree would fall over and leave a large cavity exposed by the upended root ball.

In recent years, there have been additional slumping episodes. After it moved again in 1995, SIUE did some testing on and below the slumped

An aerial view of the west side of Monks Mound showing ancient slumps and modern cracks resulting from recent slumping on the Second Terrace. *Cahokia Mounds State Historic Site.*

west side. An engineering project to stabilize the slump was activated by the State of Illinois, which included adding bentonite into the exposed cracks at the scarp, covering the filled area with geotechnical fabric and then placing additional soil over that to soften the contours of the slump scarp. Additionally, a low earthen berm was constructed above the failure zone to divert surface water away from the large crack to avoid lubricating it.

A new technology of horizontal boring was employed to install drains into the failed area to extract water, which was the basic culprit causing the slumping, as this was believed to be the least invasive and destructive method to try to resolve this problem. Five borings were placed from the ground level at the base of the mound and up into the failed slump area. With this technology, the end of the drill can be manipulated to go up, down or sideways. After going into the mound a certain distance, the boring would then go upward, poking through the surface where a semiflexible and perforated drainage tube would be attached and dragged back through the hole as the borer was reversed. The five tubes then converged into a collection chamber at the base of the mound. Unfortunately, some never worked properly, and all eventually failed.

One of the borings for the southernmost drain had gone in about forty-six meters (150 feet) and was about twelve meters (40 feet) below the surface of the Second Terrace. At that point, the drill operator said that he was drilling through stone and it felt like cobbles or slabs about a foot in size, based on work he had done elsewhere. He went through about ten meters (32 feet) of the stones, and when he began to back out the drill, the $5,000 drill bit with its electronic sensor (to track it from the surface) broke off and is now embedded in the stone mass. (It will be interesting to see how archaeologists of the future might interpret that item! Hopefully, the documentation of the project will survive until that time.) At this point in time, we do not know what this stone mass represents. A tomb? A ceremonial platform? A structure of some type? All we know is that it goes at least 32 feet in one direction (northwest–southeast); we don't know how thick it is or how wide an area it covers. We know it does not occur under the whole mound, as no vertical cores have ever encountered stone. In fact, in all of the excavations at Cahokia, we have not encountered stone structures except the one on the east slump (see the next section). There are lots of smaller stones and an occasional slab of limestone or sandstone but nothing like this. This stone mass is probably limestone, and the closest sources would be sixteen to twenty-four kilometers (ten to fifteen miles) from Cahokia, so it had to be used for something special. Remote sensing tests were not able to penetrate deep enough to determine the size of this mass, but hopefully in the near future some seismic sounding tests will determine its dimensions. Attempts at using a hand bucket auger to get down to it vertically were unsuccessful after encountering a hard, densely packed layer of dark clay, possibly an old mound surface. In fact, the hole filled up with water fairly rapidly—the auger hole must have tapped into a perched water table within the mound.

Whatever the reasons for the slumping, it has happened many times over the years and may result from a combination of factors rather than any one singular cause. The fact that it has occurred on several areas of the mound suggests there is a weakness in the integrity of the mound that can be set off periodically. Perhaps it is the interfacing of different soil types or construction stages that provides a weak point as one slides across the other when lubricated by moisture or other conditions.

THE EAST LOBES

Another project by Melvin Fowler and the UWM was the East Lobes project directed by Ken Williams in 1971. The East Lobes are two projections at the base of the east side of Monks Mound. They show up on early illustrations and maps of the mound. Fowler wanted to determine if they were the result of slumping, ramps to an earlier stage of the mound or some intentional addition to that side. A north–south trench was placed in front of the southern lobe, and an east–west trench led into the lobe. In the north–south trench, a complex series of stratigraphic zones revealed portions of houses and pits that were pre-mound features at the deepest point, mostly Late Woodland in age. Cutting through that was a wall trench paralleling the east side of the mound that looked large enough for a substantial wall or screen, which may have run around the mound or possibly served as a trap for some of the siltation coming down the mound slope. A 1.5-meter (5-foot) zone of thin layers of silt slopewash was immediately above the Late Woodland zone, apparently the result of soil washing down during rainstorms when the mound was under construction, perhaps even during the full number of years it was built, used and enlarged many times, as indicated by the ceramics found in the various layers.

Above the silt were several occupation layers with materials dating to Moorehead and Sand Prairie phases, late in the Cahokia sequence. The halting of the siltation may signal the completion of the mound or that its surface was stabilized in some way. Thus, in this one excavation, there was a fairly complete stratigraphic and chronological sequence of occupation at Cahokia, and this information was used to help establish a ceramic chronology for the site in the 1970s, although this has become more refined in more recent years. In the east–west excavation trench going into the lobe, the soil profiles showed clear evidence of classic basket loading ranging from very light tan and gray to very dark gray colors, indicating different borrow sources or different soil layers in the borrow location. There were also some fissures and other distortions of the soil, as well as what appeared to be a ditch with some human remains covered by a ridge or possible buttress near the bottom. Williams's initial interpretation was that the lobe was an intentional construction covering all of these other features, but that interpretation changed, as we will see later.

During the East Lobe excavation, while straightening up a vertical profile wall, the excavators uncovered a sandstone tablet with a diamond-shaped crosshatch pattern. A few other similar crosshatched tablets had been found at Cahokia in the past, so it was of interest but not too unusual. Later, when the tablet was being removed and Williams turned it over, he was shocked to see the engraved figure of a birdman. The figure appeared to be wearing a raptor mask with a hooked nose/beak, probably representing a falcon, holding a wing to one side in a dancing posture. I recall Williams excitedly taking the tablet around to all of the digs going on (there were five that summer) and giving out rubbings of the design. This design was eventually adopted as the official logo for Cahokia because of its uniqueness. In fact, it can be seen in a large concrete format on the overpasses over Interstate 255 as it passes through the American Bottom. The symbolism embodied on the tablet is subject to interpretation, but it is generally believed that the three spiritual realms are represented—the Upperworld by the falcon/raptor; the Middle World by the man wearing the regalia; and the Underworld by the crosshatching, which is representative of snakeskin. It is unclear how such a tablet would be used, whether it was displayed or worn in some way, used for stamping designs on clothing or bodies or served a more practical function. Some fanciful theories abound as well, but birdman symbolism is a hallmark of the Mississippian and is seen in various forms on stone, shell, copper and ceramic artifacts.

In 1984, the northern East Lobe formed a crack near the top of the slope, and the whole lobe began moving slowly downward and pushing outward like an earthen glacier. The Illinois State Museum was contracted to test the slump area, and Michael Wiant and Chip McGimsey came down to do the

"Stupendous" Monks Mound

Above: The excavation unit in the
southern East Lobe of Monks
Mound shows clear evidence of
basket loads of different colored soils.
The fifty-centimeter string grid is
used for mapping purposes. *University
of Wisconsin–Milwaukee, Archaeological
Research Laboratory.*

Left: The Cahokia Birdman Tablet,
engraved sandstone, found in the
East Lobes excavations on Monks
Mound in 1971. The design has
been adopted as the logo for Cahokia
Mounds. *Pete Bostrom photo.*

work. In the trenches they dug, they were able to identify the slip face, called a "slickenside," and could see that it penetrated deep into the mound. This was not a surface erosion but a large hunk of the mound moving as a mass. An engineering firm was contracted to examine ways to stabilize or fix the slump and to extract five cores from the mound—three on top, one in the slump and another off the north side of the mound. The ISMS test trenches revealed soil signatures that were very similar to what Williams had seen in the southern lobe, and he eventually revised his interpretation of the south lobe being an intentional construction to one that it was also the result of an ancient slumping episode and that the human remains may have been swept off a small platform mound by the advancing slump.

The cores they extracted did not conform greatly to those of Reed, Bennett and Porter, and they did not see the proliferation of limonite bands in the new cores, although there were some other correlations in soil types. Mikels Skele, in his book on Monks Mound, *The Great Knob*, was able to see some correspondence between the two sets of cores where building stages were suggested but commented that more evidence would be desirable.

In 1985, additional soil was placed at the base of the north lobe slump to buttress it against further movement, and plastic sheeting anchored by tires was placed over the upper part of the slump area to deter water intrusion. The engineering solutions presented (about twenty of them) were not acceptable, as most would impact the mound more than the slump did, and it was decided to take a passive approach and see what happened to the mound. It did stabilize and stopped moving on its own. Eventually, in 1988, there was a fortuitous donation by the Department of Transportation of loess soil from the bluffs that had been used for temporary ramps for a nearby bridge project. They hauled in the soil and used large bulldozers to push it up into the depression in the upper part of the slump. However, they were not able to get to the top of the scarp, leaving some area exposed. Still, the slump stabilized for nearly twenty years.

RECENT SLUMPING

The east slump reactivated again in 2005. This and the other slumping episodes usually followed some very wet years, or several successive wet years, and the buildup of internal water in the mound weakened its sides. As the slope failed this time, it was eating away closer to the top of the mound.

Strewn layers of different colored soils seen in an exposure during slump repairs on the northwest corner of Monks Mound. Note the fault crack displacing the alignment of the layers. *Cahokia Mounds State Historic Site.*

There was another minor slump on the northwest corner of the mound that was more of a shallow surface slump, and the west slump also dropped a few more feet along the old failure line we had repaired; it expanded farther to the north. However, it was not threatening the top of the mound like the northwest and east slumps were. We knew something had to be done as the scarp at the top of the east slump continued to calve and eat toward the top in 2007. We reviewed several possible solutions—such as driving pilings or pins into it, capping it over with clay, building a large berm around it, stone columns, etc.—but, as before, most of these would have had serious effects on the mound, more than the slumping.

It was decided to use power equipment to remove the fill from the previous repair on the east side, as well as any slumped soil, since it was all displaced, and to cut step-like terraces into the stable mound. Next, geotechnical grid material would be laid down on each terrace and new clay soil would be deposited in one-foot layers and compacted. This process would be repeated until the exposed area was filled. All this time,

Photography, surveying and soil sampling of excavations on the slump repairs on the east side of Monks Mound in 2007. Note some of the different soil zones exposed. *Cahokia Mounds State Historic Site.*

the work was monitored by archaeologists. Some fascinating soil profiles were exposed in both the northwest and east cuts. Many contrasting layers of light and dark, coarse- and fine-grained soils could be observed. Slip faults could be seen, as well as old erosional gullies that had been repaired. Basket-load lenses and sod block layers were visible in several locations. Due to the size of the exposed surfaces and the complex stratigraphy, a call went out to local archaeologists to assist with the mapping, photography, soil sampling and other tasks, and dozens of people toiled for two weeks in blazing August heat (over one hundred degrees for much of the time) to document this chance of a lifetime to see into part of Monks Mound, even though it was just a small part of one side. Time was of the essence, as we did not want to have this large area open and subject to rain damage and we needed to fill it in as soon as possible. Fortunately, it did not rain during that time. John Kelly, T.R. Kidder and Tim Schilling, all from Washington University, directed the project. Numerous archaeologists also visited during the project, some even staying to assist. Hundreds of photos were taken, and over two hundred soil samples were collected, indicating that most of the soils were coming from organically rich wetland sediments, probably the Edelhardt meander scar where Cahokia Creek and Canteen Creek once flowed just north of Monks Mound.

An interesting feature was encountered about halfway up the east exposure. One end of a limestone "platform" was exposed, consisting of small to large limestone slabs (one estimated at over forty pounds) scattered over what was probably a former edge of the mound. It had been scattered by ancient slump and erosion episodes and the overburden of the mound fill above it. There were also two sections of logs or posts within this feature that have been identified as bald cypress. It is not clear if they were vertical at one time, but they could have been posts for a roof over the slab floor, creating a chamber, or it may have just been a platform and the logs had some other function. Not enough was revealed to make that determination since only one end of the feature was exposed and we don't know how far back into the mound it goes or its total shape or size. The stone was left in place, except for a couple of samples removed for analysis. Whether this stone feature is anything similar to the one under the west side is unclear at this time. We know that they are not connected since they are at different elevations, and as noted before, cores drilled through the mound in several locations did not encounter any stone.

The repairs on the east and northwest slumps have held well, even though 2008 and 2009 were two of the wettest years on record for our area. Time will be the true test for those areas. It is possible that there will be future slumps there or in adjacent areas, but those problems will be addressed as needed.

The Mysteries of Mound 72

A small, inconspicuous mound about seven feet (2.1 meters) high sits about a half mile (0.8 kilometers) south of behemoth Monks Mound. It did not appear on most of the maps made of Cahokia. However, it turned out to be one of the most significant mounds ever excavated in North America, providing intriguing glimpses into the customs and beliefs of Mississippian peoples.

When Melvin Fowler examined the new maps he had commissioned in 1966 for Cahokia, he began looking for possible alignments, placements and indications of community planning and began drawing lines between mounds to see if any patterns were evident. One of the patterns that emerged was an equilateral triangle in the center of the site connecting the southernmost mounds in two sets of small twin mounds, Mounds 68 and 62, with its apex at the southwest corner of the First Terrace of Monks Mound. Bisecting this triangle, Fowler developed his north–south centerline for the site, essentially dividing the site in half. He thought the Mississippians had probably done something similar, and if so, they would probably have marked spots with posts where the centerline crossed mounds or intersected other lines.

One point crossed by the centerline was the southeast end of the small Mound 72. It was a ridgetop mound and sat at a different angle than the other mounds—120 degrees south of north—which, as Warren Wittry had pointed out to Fowler, happens to align with the winter solstice sunrise and summer solstice sunset at this latitude. This would be important in some of Fowler's later interpretations of Mound 72 and Cahokia.

The Mysteries of Mound 72

Mound 72 is a small ridgetop mound about forty-two meters (140 feet) long and twenty-one meters (70 feet) wide that covered three smaller mounds built over high-status and sacrificial burials. *Cahokia Mounds State Historic Site.*

In 1967, Fowler began excavations of Mound 72. He had selected it because of its small size, its unique orientation and the fact that it was one of the few ridgetop mounds. It was also on state property, which meant that he did not have to go through complex negotiations with private landowners. While pondering over his maps and alignments, he decided to dig at the southeast end, as he thought that the point where the centerline crossed might be marked by a large post. His crew began digging where he told them to but did not find a post. Fowler was sure that there should be something there and went back to his maps and calculations. He soon realized he had made a simple mathematical error. He went back to the site and had them move about three meters and dig a new trench. There, they revealed a large circular dark stain—the predicted post pit. It is rare in archaeology to find something that you have predicted, and as the dig progressed, they found many things Fowler had not predicted. The surprises continued over five seasons of excavations, from 1967 to 1971, including the discovery that there were three smaller primary mounds beneath the ridgetop mound.

After finding the large post pit, the excavations continued in that area, revealing the contours of one of the primary mounds, which turned out to be a small rectangular platform mound oriented close to the cardinal

This dark circular stain represents where a tall post once stood at the location Melvin Fowler predicted there might be one to mark his proposed north–south centerline for Cahokia. *Illinois State Museum.*

directions and covered with a light-colored soil. There was also a small ramp to the west and a large post at its east side. Later analysis of the data would show that the post had been replaced two more times, and another ramp extension covered that location. Also, a small black "altar," or platform, was placed over part of the western ramp, contrasting with the whitish surface of the mound.

As the primary mound was excavated, the excavators were startled to find the burial of a man laid on a platform of some twenty thousand shell beads, made from whelk (conch) shell originating in the Gulf of Mexico. Another male of similar age and size (early forties, about six feet tall) was beneath the man on the beads. The bead platform was made in the form of a bird, probably representing a falcon, an important Mississippian motif. Around them were six more individuals. One was a bundle burial of someone who had preceded them in death and whose bones had been gathered into a bundle or basket and reburied here. The other individuals are possible retainers, who may have been sacrificed to accompany this high-status pair of men, possibly early leaders of Cahokia. One of these was lying in a splayed position with arms and legs akimbo, as if he had just been tossed there, perhaps not quite dead until reaching his final position.

Just to the southwest of the beaded burial (I use the singular here as it is probably the man on top of the beads who was the most important), and also under the primary mound (which Fowler dubbed 72Sub1), was a group of seven men and women. Heaped on this group were the offerings to the

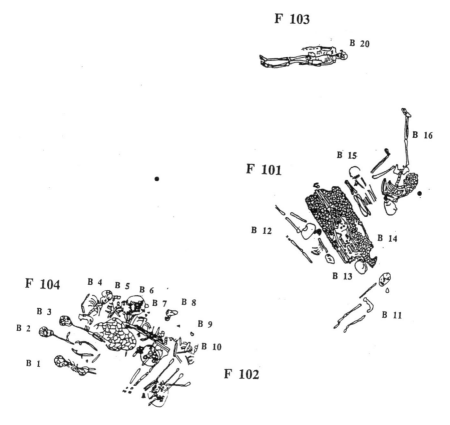

The Mound 72 beaded burial group and the grave good cache group were surface burials under 72Sub1 primary mound. *Illinois State Museum.*

The cache of artifacts included fifteen chunkey stones, a large pile of mica, meter-long rolls of copper, marine shell beads and two piles totaling 745 arrow points laid on top of seven men and women, apparently in tribute to the "beaded burial." *Illinois State Museum.*

beaded burial. This included nearly two bushels of mica, a translucent and reflective mineral that occurs in thin layers and originates from the Smoky Mountains region of North Carolina. Normally, we feel fortunate to find one little piece of mica, which often was made into beads or bangles, sewn onto the clothing of the elite. Next to the mica were fifteen chunkey stones, or discoidals—stone discs about four inches in diameter and concave on both sides. These were used in a game that later Indians in the South called "chungke," in which two men usually competed by throwing lances or markers toward the rolling stone, attempting to have their marker land closest to it and thus scoring points (see "The Grand Plaza and Its Mounds"). It is rare to find one, but to find fifteen together is unique. Most of the chunkey stones were made of a quartzite material, but one apparently was made of a more fragile stone that disintegrated upon discovery. An interesting treatise on the chunkey game was published in the September/October 2009 *Archaeology* magazine by Timothy Pauketat, detailing the important role the game played at Cahokia, how it spread to other areas and the various ways the game was played.

Near the chunkey stones, and possibly related to them, were rolls of copper about three feet long. The condition was poor, but it appeared that there were at least two, and possibly three, rolls of sheet copper that probably had been rolled around wooden shafts. The copper originates from around Lake Superior, and the nearly pure nuggets were repeatedly heated and pounded with stone hammers to create flat sheets, sometimes using copper rivets to join smaller sheets into larger ones. Copper was most often used to make ornaments and regalia and occasionally specialized tools. It is possible that these rolls of copper may have been ritual lances used in a ceremonial chunkey game, or they may have been held and displayed by leaders as a symbol of authority, much like a scepter held by royalty today. Strands of large shell disc beads were found adjacent to the copper staffs and may have been attached or suspended from them in some manner.

Also a part of this offering cache were two piles of arrow points, all prime examples of the flintknapper's art and apparently never used. In each pile they were all aligned with their tips in one direction—one group aligned west-northwest, with 332 points, and the other east-southeast, with 413 points. Within each pile were clusters of similar points, deposited as whole arrows with the shafts now decayed, and possibly in quivers or tied in bundles. The styles of the point clusters varied, as did the source of the chert from which they were made, showing origins in Oklahoma, Missouri, Wisconsin, Tennessee and Illinois. The beaded burial group and the grave good cache group were covered with a rectangular primary mound (72Sub1) aligned with the cardinal directions. At some later point in time, an intrusive pit was dug down to the grave cache group, and three more individuals were buried at right angles to the others.

All of these forms of exotic tribute demonstrate the extent of trade that Cahokia had with distant areas, along trade routes that were very ancient but more formalized during Mississippian times. It also demonstrates the power and authority the beaded burial had in life, as well as death, and confirms the belief in an afterlife—you could take your material possessions with you.

But the story of Mound 72 doesn't stop there. Excavations continued at the northwest end of Mound 72, where another primary mound, 72Sub2, was identified. It had a complex history of pre-mound activity, mound construction, alteration, expansion and burial groups. It appears that prior to the construction of this primary mound, and Mound 72 as a whole, there was a rectangular wall-trench structure at this location, its long axis oriented basically east to west. It was probably contemporary with the large post at the southeast end of the mound, and it is believed that this was probably a charnel house where the bodies of select deceased Cahokians were stored until the proper time for burial. This is indicated by the presence of the

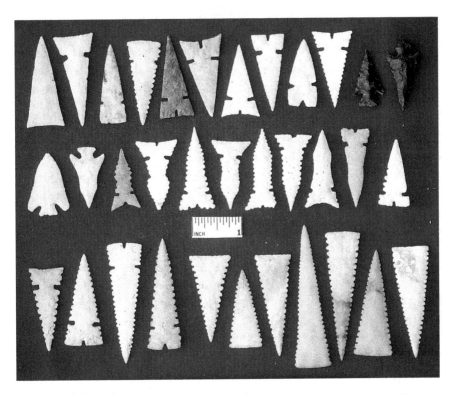

Above: The variety of points in the two Mound 72 caches were made of chert from Missouri, Illinois, Oklahoma, Wisconsin and Tennessee. Many styles are represented, perhaps identifying the group that made them. *Cahokia Mounds State Historic Site.*

Opposite, top: A group of 332 arrow points in apparent clusters of similar types pointing east-southeast. They were probably complete arrows originally, possibly in quivers or bundles. *Illinois State Museum.*

Opposite, bottom: The second group of 413 arrow points, also in clusters, pointing west-northwest. Both groups were exquisitely chipped and never used. *Illinois State Museum.*

burials of about twenty-one individuals, placed on a low square platform built over the remains of the charnel house, mostly just above where the southern wall of the charnel house had been. Four were bundle burials, and at least thirteen people between the ages of fifteen and thirty-five were represented in "pile" burials of loose bones. Additionally, there were four extended burials oriented north–south to the south and east of the pile burials, some apparently of high status. One, probably a twenty-five- to thirty-five-year-old female, was wearing a choker or necklace of four strands of shell disc beads; next to her was a twenty-five- to thirty-five-year-old male with a five-strand bead choker, but he was lying face down. Two other males along the east edge of the building were the same age as the others and were also lying face down; one had what appeared to be a shell bead hairpiece.

Next, two burial pits were emplaced into the platform. The long axis of the one near the northeast corner was oriented north to south and contained twenty-two burials oriented east to west, piled in two layers. Those that were identifiable were females. The pit near the southwest corner was oriented east to west and contained nineteen burials oriented north to south, also in two layers. Although preservation was especially poor, it is likely that these were also female burials. Both pits had the floors lined with sand before the placement of the burials, and there were indications of mats lining the floors and walls and possibly between the burial layers. Fowler believes these two burial groups were part of ceremonies dedicated to the central group at the charnel structure. Following these burials, the western portion of this platform was raised about eighty centimeters (2.6 feet), and it had a small ramp facing east leading to the lower terrace that was part of the original platform.

The next series of events at 72Sub2 reflects a change in the orientation of activities and features at Mound 72 from the cardinal directions to a northwest–southeast direction. A pit was dug into the southeast corner of the primary mound at the new orientation, and twenty-four women were buried there in two layers at right angles to the pit orientation, with their heads to the northeast. Mats lined the pit and covered the burials, and then a platform was built over it with ditches along the sides. The southeast end and the northwest end blended into the mound. Also, at the location of the burial pit of the nineteen women at the southwest corner of the original platform, a new pit was dug with a northwest–southeast orientation, but not down to the level of the burials. In it were placed dedicatory offerings, including over 36,600 marine shell beads—both large and small, disc- and barrel-shaped—and several whelk shells that may have been necklace pendants. Near the beads was another cache of arrow points, 451 of them, and they were not on shafts or in quivers like the piles under 72Sub1 but deposited in random order and probably in a large basket or bag. Most of the forms were similar to those seen in the 72Sub1 caches, but these were made primarily from local cherts. Scattered around these points were many bone and antler points, the latter having a harpoon-like appearance with barbs. Unfortunately, most of these were not well preserved and had crumbled to dust, except for a few of the antler points. Nearby were six broken pots that looked like they had been smashed against the edge of the pit. It was not uncommon among some American

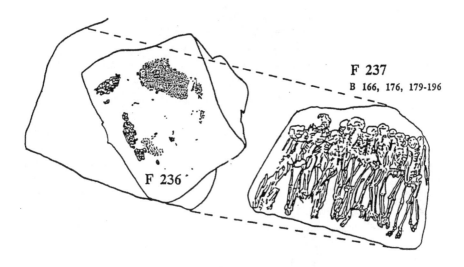

F 237
B 166, 176, 179-196

F 236

The burial pit of nineteen young women at the northwest end of Mound 72. At some later date, another pit was dug in the same location, and this upper pit had over 36,600 marine shell beads, another cache of arrow points (top) and six ceramic vessels. *Illinois State Museum.*

Indian groups to "kill" or sacrifice pottery, ostensibly to release the spirit of the vessel at the time of burial. However, the weight of the overburden of soil in Mound 72 also could have crushed them.

Excavations into the central area of the mound, between 72Sub1 and 72Sub2, revealed another primary mound, 72Sub3 (as it was later determined to be the last in the sequence of the primary mounds), a conical mound with clear evidence of basket loading. Beneath it was a unique burial. On a low prepared platform on the original surface, and at right angles to the ridgetop of Mound 72, were four men with their arms interlocked and their head area oriented to the northeast—but their heads and hands were missing, apparently cut off in some elaborate ritual. They ranged in age from twenty to forty-five years. The reason for removing the heads and hands is unclear—and they were never found—but it is not likely that this was punishment or they would not have been given this special burial in this special mound.

Next to the four men and the small mound over them was a large rectangular pit about 1.5 meters (five feet) deep, also oriented at right angles to the ridgetop mound. At the bottom of the pit were fifty-three burials laid out in two rows, two deep, oriented parallel to the ridgetop, their heads to the northwest. Only about half could be aged and sexed with some accuracy, but of those that could, most had female characteristics and an age range

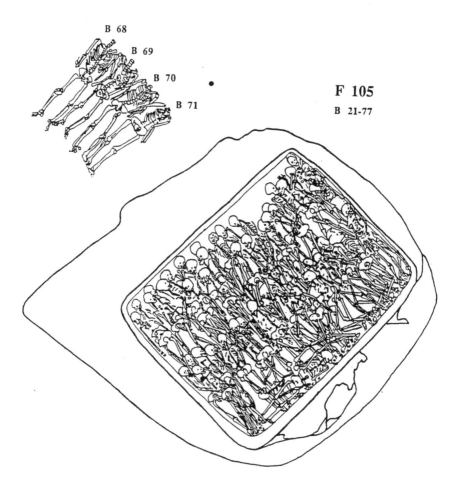

B 68

B 69

B 70

B 71

F 105

B 21-77

Above: A schematic of the burial pit with fifty-three women laid out in two rows, two deep, and the surface burial of four men with their heads and hands removed, both beneath 72Sub3 primary mound. *Illinois State Museum.*

Opposite, top: This cache of over four hundred arrow points may have been in a basket or bag. There were also numerous bone points and many harpoon-shaped points made from deer antlers. *Illinois State Museum.*

Opposite, bottom: Excavations into 72Sub3, which can be seen in the upper right profile and which covered the burial of four headless and handless men. The rectangular stain in the center turned out to be a pit containing fifty-three young women. *University of Wisconsin–Milwaukee, Archaeological Research Laboratory.*

averaging from fifteen to twenty-five years old. The remaining ones did not exhibit male characteristics. Thus, it is presumed that all of these burials represent young women, except for one that was an older female laid at a right angle to and on top of the others along one edge of the pit. The limited age range and gender is indicative of human sacrifice, since disease is not quite that selective to such a narrow window of a population; the same is also suggested for the female burial pits in 72Sub2. Like the other pits, matting material lined the pit and covered the bodies. Fowler believed the women were a dedicatory offering to the four men above them.

A conical mound about two meters high covered this burial pit and part of the mound over the four men and was expanded to the west to form a connection to 72Sub2, creating a continuous rectilinear mound oriented northwest to southeast that was over sixty-five feet long and thirty-two feet wide, with a small terrace on the southeast end. All of this pointed toward the area of the beaded burial under 72Sub1, and Fowler suggested that this indicates that the 72Sub1 and 72Sub2 mounds and burial complexes were dedicatory offerings to and commemorations of the beaded burial group.

If all of this was not enough, additional burial pits were placed along the southwestern edge of this expanded mound. The largest one was about six feet deep, over six meters (twenty feet) long, oriented northwest to southeast and had two layers of burials oriented northeast to southwest, each quite different. The pit was first lined with white sand, and then thirty-nine males and females between the ages of fifteen and forty-five were buried there—the majority were males, but fifteen were not able to be sexed. They were apparently standing on the southern lip of the pit and were clubbed to death, falling into the pit in various positions, three face down, three on their sides and the rest on their backs. They were not respectfully placed, as seen in the other burial pits. A couple of them may not have died immediately, as they were lying face down with their fingers digging into the pit floor; three were decapitated and one partially decapitated, probably with a heavy stone axe or mace, and the heads were placed with them. Two burials had arrow points in the body cavity area that could have been related to their death, or they may have been unrelated old war wounds.

At least two layers of matting were placed over these burials, and the upper layer of fifteen burials was placed on that. This group was also unusual in that a number of the burials had cedar poles alongside them, framework for the litters on which they had been carried there. These are often referred to as the "litter burials." The blanket or matting stretched between the poles had disintegrated. Only about six could be clearly identified by sex—one male

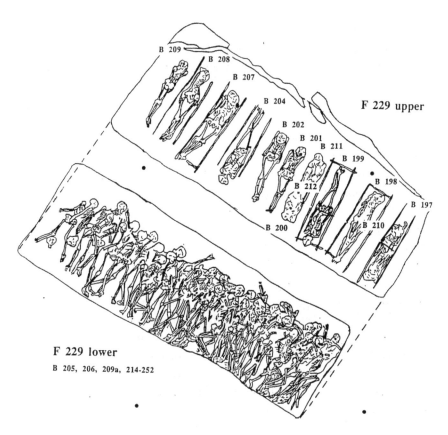

B 209
B 208
B 207
B 204
F 229 upper
B 202
B 201
B 211
B 199
B 212
B 198
B 197
B 200
B 210

F 229 lower
B 205, 206, 209a, 214-252

Double-layered burials from a pit about 1.8 meters (six feet) deep. The bottom layer had thirty-nine individuals tossed in, perhaps in violence; the upper layer contained fifteen individuals wrapped and placed on litters. Both groups had male and female burials of various ages. *Illinois State Museum.*

and five females—plus there were at least three children between six and ten years old and a juvenile between fifteen and twenty. For four of the burials, the litter poles were absent, probably decayed, so they may have been of a different wood type, but impressions for some were still visible in the soil. Most of the burials showed indications of having been wrapped, as bone tie beads were found with them and the arms/elbows were often pulled in tight to the body. One litter had an adult female and a child buried together, and another had three completely disarticulated skeletons in a pile burial. A couple of the burials had dislocated skulls, indicating that the bodies had at least partially decomposed, and one may have been decapitated. Not all of the burials had their skulls oriented in the same direction, as they were probably carried there already bound in mats or blankets, and the location of the heads may not have been visible. The relationship between these individuals is not clear, but they obviously died at different times and there had been some need to keep them together—perhaps they were kinfolk or members of the same clan, lineage or some other social group.

Also along the southwest side of the primary mounds was a series of smaller pits oriented parallel to the new orientation (northwest–southeast), including some with one or two burials and others with bundle burials. Another had eight individuals with their heads oriented to the northeast and who appear to have been bound, as bone tie beads were found at the shoulders, waist and ankles. Litter poles were not found, but the spacing between burials supports the possibility that there may have been poles that have not survived. At least one other pit was not excavated and likely held more individuals.

Following all of this, the final shaping of the mound took place, with the removal of the post and a little alteration at each end so that the ridgetop form was oriented in the proper direction. The final capping with soil created what we see as Mound 72. Even then, there was a series of intrusive extended and bundle burial pits along the southwest side, but it is not clear when these took place. In the end, a total of 272 burials were encountered in the five seasons of excavation, but there could be more in some unexcavated pits and in the northern portions of the mound that were not dug. It would probably be safe to say that there were about three hundred burials in this unique mound.

Thus, as Fowler says in his Mound 72 volume:

Even though...the dedicatory mound was finished, this area of Cahokia—and the lineage whose leaders were interred there—remained sacred and significant to some segment of Cahokia society. Representatives of that segment still paid homage to their ancestors and the power they had wielded for some generations after its early Mississippian heyday.

WOODHENGE-72?

One of the features that Fowler focuses on extensively in his writings about Mound 72 is that there is another Woodhenge located there. He was prompted to examine this theory by the research on Woodhenge alignments that Clay Sherrod and Martha Rolingson proposed (see the Woodhenge chapter) and the possibility of other Woodhenges, including one in the

Mound 72 area. Fowler was intrigued by this idea because he thought there were celestial alignments in the layout of Mound 72 and possibly its relationship to the small Mound 96 just to the southwest. The line between that mound and the big post (PP1) at the southeast end of Mound 72 is the summer solstice sunrise/winter solstice sunset alignment. Plus, the distance between them is almost identical to the diameter of Woodhenge 3, at 125 meters (410 feet).

Fowler then reexamined his excavation data to see if there were indications of other posts in Mound 72, especially at the spacing seen at Woodhenge 3. He saw evidence of dipping soil layers in one of the profiles just northwest of PP1, but that area had not been fully excavated. Another post pit (PP2) appears to have been situated near the northwest end of the mound by 72Sub2 mound and exactly where the burial pit of twenty-two females was later located. That burial pit could be seen superimposed on what appear to be the insertion/extraction pits for the post, but excavations had not extended deeper than the base of the burial pit. However, PP1, PP2 and Mound 96 all fall on the circumference of the proposed circle. Mound 72 would fit into the northeast quadrant of this circle.

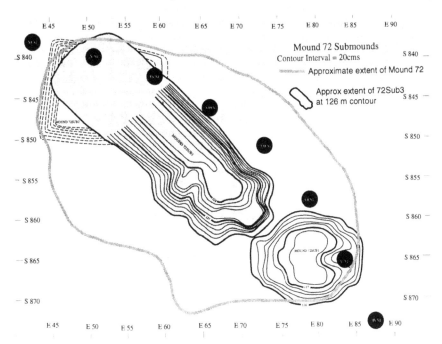

A map showing the three primary mounds in their final stages and the locations of identified (three) and proposed post pits that may be associated with a possible Woodhenge. *Illinois State Museum.*

During the 1990s, Fowler came back to explore his hypotheses more with remote sensing (electrical conductivity) and soil coring, followed by excavations. The sensing tests did reveal soil disturbances (anomalies) at or near many of the proposed post locations. The excavations did not produce clearly defined post pits like the one seen under Mound 72 or in other areas of the site, but there was definitely some human activity at these locations that disturbed the natural stratigraphy. To convince his colleagues that these were posts was a challenge for Fowler, and many of them remain unconvinced. However, he believed it and so did some of his colleagues, including Bill Gartner, a soils specialist who worked on the project. Fowler noted that one of the problems with soils in that part of the site was that they tended to "flow," or shift, especially some of the clay upper zones that dominated the area. This was observable during the earlier, as well as later, excavations under certain conditions. He contended that this would result in distortion of the man-made features, making them less recognizable to the untrained eye. Nonetheless, Fowler believed he had good evidence for six posts along the eastern arc of Woodhenge-72, three underneath Mound 72 and three others at the summer solstice, equinox and winter solstice sunrise positions. Unfortunately, a center post was not found in excavations of the center of the circle.

His interpretations of Mound 72 are greatly based on the presence of a Woodhenge there, which he called "Woodhenge-72." The beaded burial and several of the other burial pits appear to be focused on some of the proposed post locations other than the PP1, and Fowler believed the Woodhenge-72 posts were standing through most of the stages of construction and burials, until the final capping of the mound, when they were removed.

Interpreting Mound 72

Obviously, with so many unique burials in Mound 72—their positioning and alignments, the possible Woodhenge association and the exotic grave goods—there are many potential interpretations of what all of this means. Analysis of the skeletal remains shows that certain burial groups were of higher status than others and that some may have come from places other than Cahokia. The variations in burial treatment are also indicative of differing social status since, when one is treated differently in death, it reflects differences in life as well. Some people had exotic goods buried with them, as well as possible attendants; others were carefully laid in the graves on litters or in tightly wrapped coverings; still others had been moved from other locations to join their kin at this sacred space, their bones wrapped in bundles; and others appear to have been dispatched in violence and tossed into a grave with little respect.

Some features were aligned with the cardinal directions and others to the angles of important sunrises and sunsets and other directional markers, and the burial pits and the bodies in them are similarly aligned. This did not happen all at once but in a series of episodes over an unknown span of time, mostly during the early stages of Cahokia's explosive expansion around AD 1050. Many episodes appear to have been commemorative events focusing on certain structures or burial groups, maintaining the honor and memory of those who had passed on before.

Currently, there are several archaeologists who see much of the activity at Mound 72 as a form of theatre—public display and ceremony reflecting their belief system, mythology and cosmology. James Brown, Timothy Pauketat, Julie Holt and Alice Kehoe, to name a few, have written about their interpretations of what Mound 72 may represent, searching for meaning to all of this mortuary display. I will not attempt to do that here as I have focused on the discovery and excavation results, but I urge those of you who want to learn more to consult some of the literature about Mound 72 so you can draw your own conclusions.

We may never know the real answers to the questions posed, but as we continue to examine the data, look at the traditions of possible descendants and tease apart the meaning of what we see, we can continue to gain insights into the mysteries of Mound 72.

The Grand Plaza and Its Mounds

At the heart of Cahokia is one of the largest communal public spaces in the Americas, appropriately in front of the largest prehistoric earthwork in the Americas. The Grand Plaza covers an area of sixteen to twenty hectares (forty to fifty acres), depending on where one draws the lines for its perimeter. It spreads from Monks Mound on the north to the Twin Mounds on the south. Its western edge is bordered by Mounds 48 and 57 and its eastern edge by Mounds 51, 50, 54 and 55. Within the plaza are Mounds 49 and 56.

This was the heart of the city and would have been as important to the Cahokians as the mounds. The Grand Plaza would have been the scene of major festivals, feasts, games, rituals, dances and possibly market activity, as well as other public gatherings. What is amazing about the Grand Plaza is that most of it is artificially created. The naturally undulating ridge and swale topography, which is typical of the flood plain, was cut and filled to create a level plain. As much as three feet of soil was deposited in some areas, less in others, and all of this was capped with sandy soil to provide secure footing. Here, the populace would assemble to hear declarations from the paramount chief on top of Monks Mound. The acoustics provided by this space and mound allowed his voice to carry across the plaza—an effect that can still be experienced today when vehicle, train and plane traffic is quiet. They could also celebrate the dedication of mounds, the ascent of new leaders, important dates in their ritual and agricultural calendar and various rites of passage.

The Grand Plaza and Its Mounds

Evidence for this massive construction came from a variety of tests. Rinita Dalan, George Holley and their colleagues from Southern Illinois University–Edwardsville (SIUE) initially conducted remote sensing tests across the Grand Plaza with electrical conductivity instruments. These indicated a buried surface in the form of what appeared to be a sandy ridge angling northwest to southeast near the middle of the plaza, with filled-in swales on either side. Excavations, commonly called "ground truthing," were then conducted to test the results of the remote sensing. These confirmed the existence of the ridge and filled-in swales and the artificial creation of the Grand Plaza. They also encountered a large post pit, where a tall post once stood, perhaps a marker post in the playing field for the game of chunkey. Although no proof of one has been found, most artists' renderings of Cahokia show a chunkey field in the Grand Plaza, as it is believed that there would have been one there.

An intriguing article by archaeologist Timothy Pauketat on this ancient game appeared in the August/September 2009 issue of *Archaeology* magazine and explored the important role that Cahokia played in the spread of this game, which was still being played by historic-period southern tribes such as the Creek and by the Mandan as far away as North Dakota. As noted in the Mound 72 chapter, usually two men would compete, rolling a concave-sided stone disc on its edge down a prepared field, running after it and launching lances to the spot where they anticipated the chunkey stone would come to rest. The closest lance would define the winner, and there was usually much wagering on the outcome by the contestants and their fans. As with most American Indian activities, there was no separation of "church and state," and it is likely there were rituals and symbolism that were part of the chunkey game. Some references indicate that the game stone, with its circular shape, was symbolic of the sun, and rolling it down the field was symbolic of the passage of the sun across the sky. The discovery of fifteen chunkey stones in an artifact cache in Mound 72 indicates the important role these objects, usually seven to ten centimeters (three to four inches) in diameter, played at Cahokia.

In the 1990s, Pauketat and colleagues Susan Alt and Jeff Kruchten, through the State University of New York–Buffalo, monitored the excavations for a new waterline at Cahokia, much of which traversed the north and central areas of the Grand Plaza. Their work further substantiated the filling and leveling of the plaza and also the general absence of residential features such as houses and pits. However, as the excavations approached the outer limits of the plaza, houses and pit features were encountered. Thus, one

A view of the Grand Plaza, looking north between the Twin Mounds toward Monks Mound in the distance. A chunkey yard is in the center with traders' booths along the edges, in front of the homes of the elite. *Lloyd K. Townsend, Cahokia Mounds State Historic Site.*

can envisage a large open space in the middle of the city of relatively bare soil, bordered by mounds of various sizes; around them were dwellings and public buildings. These were probably dwellings of some of Cahokia's elite. Some buildings may have been used only during festivals, gatherings or other public functions. At times the plaza would have been relatively vacant and, at other times, a scene of bustling activity.

The presence of two mounds (49 and 56) in the Grand Plaza and in front of Monks Mound suggests that they had some special significance. Mound 56, about twelve feet high today and probably about fifteen feet high originally, was deeply trenched, augered and had test pits dug into it by W.K. Moorehead in the early 1920s, but little information survives about what he found other than "a few scales of copper, and some fragments of a highly finished pottery." In 1993, the SIUE field school relocated Moorehead's trench with remote sensing and partially reopened it, hoping to re-expose a vertical profile. Unfortunately, one did not survive, since Moorehead had used horse-drawn slips to cut the trench. They did not continue due to time

constraints, and they did not want to excavate undisturbed areas of the mound. Rinita Dalan, George Holley and Harold Watters also used micro-mapping and a relatively new type of soil-testing technique that examines the soil particles in the slopewash around the mound. Even though this mound had been substantially plowed over for nearly one hundred years before the state acquired it, and it has been grass-covered since the late 1920s, the tests were still able to determine that Mound 56 had originally been a rectangular platform mound with a lower terrace facing north toward Monks Mound. As a platform mound, it would have had a building on it, but the nature of that structure is unknown.

Mound 49 is a low ridgetop mound, similar in size and shape to Mound 72, but with an east–west orientation. It sits directly in front of Monks Mound and is also along the same hypothesized north–south centerline as Mound 72, as proposed by Melvin Fowler. All of these facts have led to speculation about what it might contain. In 1994, Tim Pauketat, then with the University of Oklahoma, directed field school test excavations into the north and south

Left: The game of chunkey was a favorite sport of the Mississippians. Two men competed, trying to get their lances to land closest to where the disc-shaped stone stopped rolling. *Don Vanderbeek, Cahokia Mounds State Historic Site.*

Below: An aerial perspective of central Cahokia with the Grand Plaza at the center, dominated by Monks Mound on the north and the Twin Mounds on the south and bounded by smaller mounds, special structures and the homes of the elite. *William R. Iseminger, Cahokia Mounds State Historic Site.*

edges of the mound. They were able to determine that it originally had been a smaller platform mound built during the Lohmann phase and was later converted into a ridgetop mound. The excavations did not go into the central interior of the mound so it is not known if it also covered burials.

There are parallels, but differences in scale, if one compares the Grand Plaza to the Mall in Washington, D.C., with the Capitol building at one end (Monks Mound); the Lincoln Memorial at the opposite end (the Twin Mounds); other memorials within the Mall, such as the Washington Monument and the Vietnam Memorial (Mounds 56 and 49); and the sides flanked by museums and governmental buildings (Mounds 48, 57, 51, 50, 54 and 55 and ground-level structures). Public festivals, inauguration ceremonies for new leaders, parades, games and other special activities would occur in both settings, although it is less likely that political protests occurred at Cahokia. This core of the Central Ceremonial Precinct was the seat of power, government and religion for this ranked, hierarchical society. The paramount chief, his sub chiefs and a council of elders, priests and other officials made decisions that affected not just Cahokia but also the surrounding region, as well as, to some extent, the whole Mississippian world.

Around the perimeter of the Grand Plaza were mounds that varied greatly in size, from the large Twin Mounds at the south end and the substantial Mound 48 at the northwest corner to the diminutive Mound 57, just south of Mound 48. I believe that Mound 48 was the true "Monks Mound." French Trappist monks lived at the site from 1809 to 1813 and were visited by Henry Brackenridge and others, who described the cabins, chapel, refectory and other log structures as being on a mound to the west or southwest of the largest mound. This would be the mound with adequate space to support a number of structures. The monks did plant gardens, fruit trees and wheat on the big mound that was later called "Monks Mound" by local citizens, but there is no clear evidence that the monks ever built on it other than anecdotal references decades later that probably assumed they had built on the largest mound.

Bill Woods from SIUE conducted field school testing in conjunction with Robert Santlee of the University of New Mexico around Mound 48 and did some vertical coring of the mound that suggested that it may have been built in one stage. The excavations around the perimeter found little material on the plaza side and the possibility that there was an access ramp on the northeast corner. Around the southern side, the excavation units produced progressively more artifacts to the west, as well as a possible fence or screen

Community life and activities around the perimeter of the Grand Plaza, with Monks Mound in the background, chunkey players and a procession in progress in the plaza. *Michael Hampshire, Cahokia Mounds State Historic Site.*

paralleling the south side. The number of exotic materials found near the southwest corner of the mound might reflect residue from ceremonial activities taking place on the mound, or they could indicate high-status occupation near the mound.

Forming the eastern side of the Grand Plaza, from north to south, are Mounds 51, 50, 54 and 55. All were inside the limits of the stockade walls in ancient times. In more recent times, the smaller ones—Mounds 50 and 54—and also Mound 55 were plowed over. And they all were within the boundaries of the Mounds Place subdivision, a development of over sixty houses that was begun in 1941. They were mostly in the backyards of the houses but still suffered from abuse by gardens, trees, garages and other domestic activities. All but Mound 54 have had some type of excavation into them.

A University of Illinois crew working under Chuck Bareis did some salvage work on Mound 51, also known as "Persimmon Mound," in the mid-1960s, when its owner was selling it for fill. They were able to identify a couple building stages and hearths, but the most intriguing discovery was beneath the mound. They found deep layers of fill going down about ten feet. Some were layers of burned thatch, but several contained well-preserved perishable materials that are rarely recovered at the Cahokia site, or even throughout the eastern United States, unless they have been charred or carbonized by fire or found in a dry cave. People who worked on the crew remarked that they could still smell a strong garbage odor. Unusual things found included construction timbers, matting, thatch, food products such as berries that were still flexible, well-preserved animal bone and plant seeds, roots and skins, nuts and lots of insect remains. A large

Excavations in the sub–Mound 51 borrow pit revealed multiple layers of refuse deposits, many well preserved, apparently residue from feasting on the Grand Plaza. *Cahokia Mounds State Historic Site.*

number of swans was represented, but no wing bones, suggesting these may have been saved and possibly used as special fans. A tremendous number of deer bones represent thousands of deer that had been butchered for the feasting. There were also sherds from thousands of broken pots, quartz crystals, exotic arrow points, shell beads, a chunkey stone, a pipe and even a drilled alligator-tooth pendant. The interpretation is that all of these materials were deposited during or after feasts taking place in the Grand Plaza, and possibly even at its dedication in the mid-eleventh century. After the borrow pit was filled in, there was at least one structure built at the surface, and then Mound 51 was built over the southern portion of the pit. The northern portion of the filled-in pit appears to have then become part of a plaza between Mound 51 and Mound 36 to the north. This is one of many examples of "urban renewal" at Cahokia.

In 1986–87, Bob Gergen and I conducted test excavations into Mound 50, just south of Mound 51, with public field schools sponsored by the Cahokia Mounds Museum Society. One-meter-wide trenches were put into the east and south sides of this low, dome-shaped mound, which had been plowed down probably to half its height, standing about one meter high. The excavations showed that there had been structures that predated the mound, including one T-shaped building. This type of building is often believed to have had some type of special function, indicating there was some ceremonial use for this location before the mound was built. At some point, there was a localized flooding episode, as there was a layer of water-laid sand beneath the mound, and the flood may have actually stripped off some of the existing surface; there was no developed "A-horizon," or dark organic humus layer, typical of most vegetated surfaces. It is also possible that the Mississippians stripped and leveled the surface prior to the construction of the mound, as has been noted with most mound excavations at Cahokia, perhaps as part of a cleansing and dedicatory ritual. The Mound 50 excavations also revealed that at some point in its use, several large and deep pits had been dug into its surface and later filled in, and there were two deep and large post pits, one over three meters deep. These features indicate that this mound was not static but had repeated ritual usage over an unknown period of time. It also may have been one of the later mounds built at Cahokia. Although it has the low, domed appearance of a conical mound, it may have been the type that Pauketat has referred to as "rotundas," or flat-topped round mounds. Whether there was a building on top or the row of large posts continued across the mound is unknown, as the test trenches did not reach to the summit.

Mound 55, or the "Murdock Mound," was partially excavated by Harriet Smith, working for the Illinois State Museum with a WPA crew in 1941. The Mounds Subdivision construction had begun, and Smith was examining this mound before it became impacted by construction. About nine feet of the mound remained, and it had been subject to erosion and plowing over the years. She was able to identify several building stages of the mound, that it had a lower terrace projecting toward the Grand Plaza, that it had been covered with a layer of black clay and that some of its corners had been "faceted," or cut at an angle. Evidence of structures was found on its summit, and there was indication of fencing around the edge of the terrace. Of special interest was what was under and next to the mound. There were two structures, one large and circular and the other a rare cross-shaped building set in a circular basin. These would have been ceremonial structures and show that there was continued use of this sacred place from the time of the buildings through the construction and use of several stages of the mound. Smith, through some complex geometry and extension of slope angles, suggested that the mound

The Twin Mounds, as seen looking south from the top of Monks Mound and across the Grand Plaza. Mound 49 is to the right of the tree and Mound 56 is to the left of the tree, closer to Fox Mound. *Cahokia Mounds State Historic Site.*

may have been as tall as thirty-three feet, but the early maps of the site do not indicate a mound of that dimension. Smith also believed she could see a standard unit of measure of sixteen and a half feet (5.03 meters) used in the construction of the mound, or multiples or fractions of that amount.

All four of the above mounds were wholly or partially reconstructed in 1988 by the Illinois Department of Transportation, using distinctive yellow loess soil from the Illinois bluffs so that the new mound fill would be distinctive from any remnants of the original mounds. Also, before the new dirt was added, slabs of concrete from sidewalks in the former subdivision were scattered in the footprint of these mounds to further delineate the new from the old mounds. The locations of the former Mound 51 and Mound 55 were scaled off of a map of the site so that their basal dimensions would approximate the original, although with Mound 51 we had to hedge a little on the north side due to utility corridors and highway right of way concerns. The slope angles were also reduced to facilitate mowing, so the summits appear smaller and narrower than the original ones on these two mounds.

Mounds 50 and 54 still survived as low bumps in the terrain about a meter (3.3 feet) high, but they also were added to in order to bring them up to what are believed to be close to the original heights (2 to 3 meters) based on the old maps of the site and descriptions in Fowler's *Cahokia Atlas.*

At the south end of the Grand Plaza are the "Twin Mounds," or Fox Mound (Mound 60) and Roundtop Mound (Mound 57). They are the second tallest mounds after Monks Mound, at about 13.3 meters (forty-five feet) high. As was noted in the chapter "A City of Mounds," the Twin Mounds shared a common platform, and they may have been a mortuary complex, with a charnel structure on Fox Mound and possibly burials in Roundtop Mound. But again, without excavations to confirm that, this is speculation. However, if they are mortuary mounds, their placement in opposition to Monks Mound, which was the seat of power, order, life and the Upperworld, would seem to represent death, darkness, disorder and the Underworld. These are not necessarily positive and negative concepts but parallel ones representing balanced components of their belief system.

Other Plazas, Mounds and Structures

In this chapter, I will not attempt to describe all of the other mounds but primarily those that are associated with plazas, those that occur in what are thought to be formal groupings or those that have had some significant excavations or other testing. Even so, some will be omitted. I refer the reader to Melvin Fowler's *Cahokia Atlas*, 1997 revised edition, for more detailed descriptions of each mound and archaeological research at the site. Some of the research discussed in this chapter has taken place since the publication of Fowler's book, so besides being a summary, it is also an update for some of these site features.

Although the Grand Plaza dominates the Cahokia site, it was just one of several, although the others were not nearly as large. There were other plazas around Monks Mound: the North, East and West Plazas. These basically formed a cross of unequal arms with Monks Mound at the center. The cross in Mississippian symbolism is representative of the four cardinal directions, or the four quarters of the Earth, and is often depicted on artifacts as a circle with the cross inside. Several archaeologists believe this concept is implied by the positioning of the plazas around Monks Mound, an earthen representation of their cosmology. Most of central Cahokia was organized in relation to Monks Mound and by these plazas and their attendant mounds, which defined their borders. For the most part, plazas were open spaces without dwellings, although there might have been important special-function structures that were used for both public and ritual gatherings. It appears that most plazas were built before the erection of the stockade,

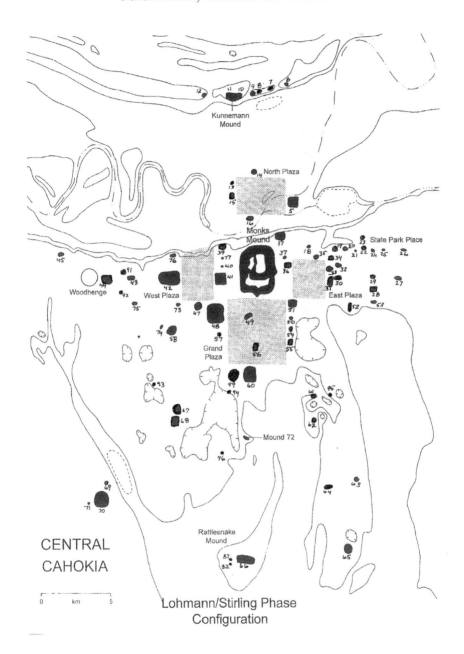

A map of central Cahokia showing the distribution of mounds and the four major plazas in early Cahokia. *Adapted from J. Kelly.*

Many of the mounds of Cahokia are laid out on north–south and east–west axes centered on Monks Mound. *Lloyd K. Townsend, Cahokia Mounds State Historic Site.*

or prior to AD 1175. Like the Grand Plaza, this configuration of plazas could date to the Lohmann phase, when Cahokia was undergoing its major expansion around AD 1050, although some may have had their start a little earlier. After the erection of the stockade, at least the East Plaza was reconfigured, and this may be true of the others as well.

NORTH PLAZA

The North Plaza and its complement of mounds is sometimes called the Creek Bottom Group, since it is located in the Cahokia Creek bottom. This plaza is bordered by Mounds 5, 13, 14, 15 and 16. Today, this plaza is bracketed by Interstate 55/70 on the south and the Canteen Creek Canal and levee on the north (both creeks were canalized and straightened out about 1916 to control drainage in the bottoms, and these two canals merge into one just west of the North Plaza). This is the lowest part of the Cahokia site, and it is likely that the bases of these mounds are buried in alluvial sediments deposited by Canteen Creek and Cahokia Creek, which at one time merged just east of the plaza and ran through the southern part of the plaza. Their location suggests that they may have been built during a drier period, when the creek bottom was not so wet, but they also may have had some relationship to the creek, possibly being used as a sort of "docking" area for the dugout canoes to beach and unload and where visitors were screened before being allowed to enter the site—sort of a port of entry. Perhaps the Cahokia elite bargained with foreign traders here for exotic items and prestige goods. Martin Byers proposes an unusual alternate theory that during times of flooding these mounds would appear to be rising from the symbolic "primordial sea" and be part of world renewal rituals. There may well be some symbolism in the placement of this plaza and its mounds, but it can only be conjectured at this time, although Kelly and Brown also suggest that this plaza and its wetland setting could be symbolically important in that it "is from this watery world that life often arises. It is from this area that we suspect that mud was taken to create Monks Mound."

Early maps of this mound group show some discrepancies in the placement of the mounds and their dimensions. The biggest one is the rectangular platform at the east side of the plaza—Mound 5—and it originally may have been 7.6 meters (twenty-five feet) tall. Its north side was partially eroded by Cahokia Creek, and in the early 1960s, during highway salvage operations for Interstate 55/70, the Illinois State Museum dug a stratigraphic trench into the north side. The other mounds have been plowed down over many years, greatly reducing their size. Mound 13 is

Elites bartering on the North Plaza for exotic prestige goods brought by traders from distant places, arriving in dugout canoes on Cahokia Creek. *Michael Hampshire, Cahokia Mounds State Historic Site.*

no longer visible in relief, but it has shown up as a soil stain in some aerial photographs. Mound 14 is now a slight rise in the field, with an elongated east–west axis, and was described in the 1880s as a conical mound about 3 meters (ten feet) high with an oval base. Moorehead trenched this mound in 1922, when it was only 1.5 meters (five feet) high, finding only some pieces of stone and bone and no pottery.

Mound 16, directly south of Mound 14, today is 0.7 meters (2.3 feet) tall, but old maps indicate that it may have been 3.0 meters (10.0 feet) tall. Although today the mound area is heavily wooded, it was originally plowed over for many years and, as late as the 1970s, was still being farmed. Mound 15 shows a little relief at 0.4 meters (1.3 feet) but also may have been around 3.0 meters tall in the 1880s. Its long axis runs north to south. Collectors have reported finding a fair amount of Hixton silicified sandstone, a granular, quartzite-like material that is known to originate in southwestern Wisconsin and from which some arrow points and other artifacts were manufactured at Cahokia.

WEST PLAZA

To the west of Monks Mound are Mounds 39, 77, 40 and 41, which marked the eastern edge of the West Plaza. The western edge may have extended as far as Mound 42 (Merrell Mound) and Mound 76; the northern edge was determined by the edge of the southern bank of the Cahokia Creek bottom (and former Edelhardt meander); and at the southern edge were Mounds 48, 47 and 73. During the early 1960s, the Illinois State Museum conducted extensive excavations in a part of this plaza complex called Tract 15-B. This salvage work preceded the relocation of Sand Prairie Lane west of its former location and its overpass over Interstate 55/70. Numerous large structures and pits were found, but the most intriguing features are what have been called the "compounds." There is a sequence of construction of these large architectural features. The initial compound was a large circular wall trench structure about fifteen meters (forty-nine feet) in diameter, followed by another larger circular structure twenty-four meters (seventy-nine feet) in diameter that may have been replaced a couple times, the final one having small circular bastions. Large posts near the center may be associated with these structures.

Next, there were two large rectangular structures built over the location of the round compounds, but exact dimensions could not be determined as the west side was outside of the highway right of way excavation area. Although

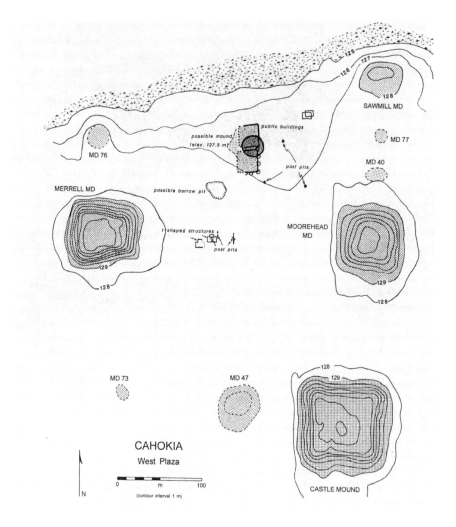

The West Plaza and its associated mounds. *Adapted from J. Kelly.*

they were next to each other, it is not clear if they were contemporary or sequential in construction. Each had small circular bastions; the north one appeared to have one centered along each wall, and the south one had corner bastions, as well as two along the side walls, based on the appearance of the east wall.

There is much conjecture about these compounds and their functions. Were they roofed over? If so, one would expect to see clear evidence of regularly spaced interior roof support posts. Plus, the amount of span for rafters would be difficult to support for structures that large. As to function,

Excavation of several superimposed Mississippian houses on the Merrell Tract portion of the West Plaza by Beloit College. *Cahokia Mounds State Historic Site.*

it is obvious that these were special places, perhaps sacred ritual enclosures, marketplaces, training grounds for warriors (suggested by the presence of bastions) or an enclave for visiting dignitaries. The general absence of houses or other structures within the compounds argues against some interpretations, although one large structure—possibly a temple, granary, council lodge or building serving some other sacred or secular purpose—may have existed inside one of them. Whatever the function of the compounds, they were built to protect what happened inside and perhaps to screen those activities from the eyes of the unprivileged.

The Merrell Tract, just west of Tract 15-B, was also part of the West Plaza. Beloit College field schools, under the direction of Robert Salzer, dug there for several years in the late 1960s and early 1970s, hoping to find evidence of the western portion of the stockade, but they were unsuccessful. However, they did find a complex sequence of house construction, large posts and two large, T-shaped structures. The latter were as much as four times larger than the typical houses, and each had a narrow anteroom extension along one of the long walls, giving them the "T" shape. Their purpose is unknown, but John Kelly suggests that since they were in the plaza, and due to their large size and special shape, they may indicate the residence of a religious specialist or some type of storehouse. Other T-shaped structures have been found at Cahokia and other sites, but they are not very common and, in most cases, are thought to have a special function, such as being used as meeting places, storage buildings for sacred items or the homes of local dignitaries or religious leaders. Most of the structures in the plaza seem to be from the Lohmann and Stirling phases, superimposing some earlier Emergent Mississippian dwellings, although it appears to have reverted to residential usage during the Moorehead phase and some construction continued into the Sand Prairie phase.

The mounds around the West Plaza vary greatly in size. Merrell Mound (Mound 42), a large rectangular platform mound at the west edge of the plaza, stands 7.6 meters (25 feet) high, 79 by 122 meters (260 by 400 feet) at the base and was oriented east to west. It once had a smaller oval platform mound about 23 meters (75 feet) in diameter on its southwest corner. Apparently that was removed by one of the occupants of the farmhouse that was built on the summit of the mound in the late 1800s. A graded driveway to the top angled up the east side, and a barn cut into part of the east base of the mound. Elizabeth Benchley of UWM trenched the area of the secondary mound as part of her research on secondary mounds, which included her work on the First Terrace of Monks Mound.

Little is known about Mound 76 at the northwest corner of the plaza, other than it was a low, square platform mound on the south edge of the bank of the marshy area of the Cahokia Creek bottom.

Along the east side of the West Plaza were four mounds. At the northeast corner of the plaza is Mound 39, also called Sawmill Mound since there was a sawmill on it in the mid-1800s that blew up, killing several workers. They may have been buried in Mound 73 or Mound 47 at the south end of the West Plaza. In the early 1920s, Moorehead dug several trenches and pits in this platform mound, which was originally about two and one-half meters (eight feet) high and on the south bank of Cahokia Creek bottom. He found eight burials on the south side, one with a shell gorget, three ceramic vessels and a bone knife. Elsewhere, a mussel shell had been carved into the form of a human face. Auger tests showed that there were apparently several building stages and layers of dark and yellow soil.

Just south of Mound 39 is Mound 77, and Moorehead believed that there was a long platform connecting this small mound to Mound 39. It may have been conical or oval in form, but it does not show on most early maps, and those that do show it are not consistent in details other than location. Today, it is only a couple feet high. Moorehead found a burned clay-lined pit with a large lump of fire-blackened galena (lead ore) weighing eight pounds and about a quart of powdered galena. Next to it was a bowl and a plate, an engraved stone and a crucible-like jar.

Continuing south was Mound 40, which is no longer visible; it only appears on the Moorehead map and an earlier one called the Ramey Map. No known excavations have taken place there. Next is Mound 41 (Moorehead Mound), a large square platform mound approximately five to six meters (seventeen to twenty feet) tall. Although it is believed that Mound 48 (Castle Mound) was where the Trappist monks lived in the early 1800s, there is a possibility that it could have been Mound 41. However, Mound 48 has the larger surface on the summit and would have better accommodated the many cabins the monks had. No known excavations have taken place in Mound 41.

South of the West Plaza were two mounds—Mound 73 and Mound 47. Unfortunately they were lost when the Falcon Drive-In Theatre was built at that location in the early 1950s and they were leveled for the entry and exit roads, although slight bumps are still visible. The earliest maps showing Mound 47 indicate that it was a small, irregularly shaped mound over three meters (ten feet) tall. No excavations took place that are known, although this may be where some of the men killed in the sawmill explosion on Mound 39 were buried. Oscar Schneider, a local collector, mentioned that when the mound was being destroyed, a large hoe, some cedar posts and other artifacts were revealed. He donated that hoe to the museum back in the 1970s. Mound 73 shows even smaller on most early maps, with a height of one and a half to three and a half meters (five to ten feet). It may have been a small conical mound, but that is unclear as both it and Mound 73 were plowed down quite a bit before they were destroyed. Moorehead said that it was elongated with an east–west axis.

EAST PLAZA

The East Plaza apparently was a more dynamic plaza, with its location changing over time. Initially, there was a plaza in the Ramey field immediately east of Monks Mound, indicated by controlled surface collections by UWM. Analyses of the material distribution by Barbara Vander Leest and Elizabeth

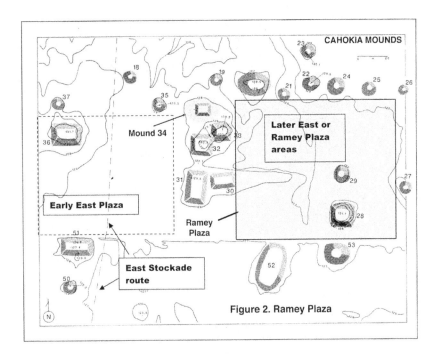

Figure 2. Ramey Plaza

Projected locations of the early and late East Plazas. The exact limits vary depending on which mounds formed its boundaries. A sunken area between Mounds 33 and 24 may represent one configuration. *Adapted from J. Kelly.*

Benchley showed very few artifacts in the area between Mound 51 and Mound 36, suggesting a plaza there, with Monks Mound on the west and the eastern extent unknown due to modern houses and other buildings in that direction. After the stockade was built around the central precinct, the East Plaza moved farther east, outside the wall. Various Cahokia researchers have indicated different interpretations of the relocated East, or Ramey, Plaza, but generally it includes areas bounded by Mounds 30, 31, 32, 33, 34, 19, 20, 21 29, 28 and 52. There is a sunken area east of Mounds 33 and 34 that tends to support the idea of a plaza there. It is also possible that it could have an eastern extension in the area between Mounds 21, 24, 25, 26, 27 and 29. These interpretations are based primarily on the linear arrangements of those mounds that seem to form rectangular patterns.

Most of these mounds were plowed over during the years when property was farmed and were reduced from their original dimensions. When local floods ripped through that part of the site in the mid-1940s and mid-'50s, the Ramey family, which still owned the land, scraped soil from some of the mounds to fill in washed-out areas, especially from Mound 33, which may have been nine meters (thirty feet) tall originally. Other mounds, specifically Mounds 30 and 31, were essentially destroyed by the construction of Grandpa Pidgeon's Discount Store about 1960. Mound 29 had a house built on it; several others were impacted by houses, streets and other construction in the State Park Place subdivision; and a trailer park still sits atop Mound 52.

In the early 1920s, Moorehead trenched a number of these mounds. Mound 30 was an east–west oriented platform mound that sat at right angles to the north half of Mound 31 to its west. Height estimates vary from 1.5 meters (five feet) to 6.1 meters (twenty feet) on the early maps. When Moorehead saw it, it was five feet high. He put a couple of long trenches into this mound and some test pits up to ten feet deep. He also found layers of debris and broken artifacts at about the seven-foot level and a burned floor below the baseline of the mound, possibly a pre-mound burned house or ceremonial structure.

Mound 31 was a north–south oriented platform mound about 7.6 meters (twenty-five feet) high. It apparently had a root cellar dug into it and later a pavilion or grandstand on top, associated with a tavern and nightclub that once stood next to it. When Grandpa Pidgeon's store was planned for construction, the Illinois State Museum sent Joseph Caldwell to do some test excavations. His work revealed numerous building stages and pre-mound village features covering most of the span of Cahokia's development. These two mounds were then leveled; however, it appears that portions of the bases of these two mounds may still be extant as low rises at the west end of the building and under its annex. The state recently acquired this property and removed the annex and several other minor structures. It awaits funding for the demolition of the main building and the floor slab of the annex. Following some archaeological research, the plans are to restore Mounds 30 and 31 and create a green space that will improve the appearance and approach to the historic site.

Moorehead also trenched several of the mounds along the north side of the East Plaza, putting a 250-foot trench through Mounds 19, 20 and 21 and testing 24 and 25. However, there is confusion with his identification of these mounds by number, and it is not always clear in his incomplete records which mound he was digging. Nevertheless, in the area of Mounds 19 and 20 he found burials, probably at the base of the mounds, accompanied by pottery, mussel shells, powdered galena and chert tools. Some of the burials, mostly women, had horizontally filed teeth, which some researchers point to as possibly showing Mesoamerican connections, as tooth filing was not uncommon in that area. However, this is still inconclusive.

Mound 34 had test units put into it by Albert Spaulding of the University of Michigan in 1950, and in 1956 Gregory Perino, working for the Gilcrease Foundation in Tulsa, conducted a major excavation into the north side of this mound. These excavations produced interesting information and artifacts associated with the Caddoan region and the Southeastern Ceremonial Complex (SECC), such as fragments of engraved marine whelk shell like those found at Spiro Mounds in Oklahoma, arrow points more commonly found in the Arkansas/Oklahoma area and some negative painted pottery. There were also chert effigy shark teeth that may have been part of a war club, along with real sharks' teeth, fragments of a burned bowl and a variety of other interesting items. Many of these came from a burned area at the juncture of a terrace on this mound. Carbon-14 dates from the burned zone seem to establish Mound 34 as one of the later mounds built at Cahokia, around AD 1290.

James Brown and John Kelly were intrigued by all of these exotic items and late dates and decided to reopen some of Perino's excavations, which had not been well documented with detailed maps. There was also limited photography. They spent eleven seasons on this project and identified the limits of most of Perino's trenches; re-exposed several of his profiles, as well as new ones; and made detailed maps of the mound stratigraphy. There is a heavy debris-laden layer that is part of the early mound construction, probably soil removed from a former borrow pit filled with refuse just north of the mound. Mound stages or additions were visible, and it appears that this was a platform mound with a building on top and a terrace around at least three, and possibly all four, sides. Brown and Kelly believe the burned zone that Perino found was a result of the building on top being burned and the debris, including a lot of the items that were in the building, being pushed over the side onto the terrace. Throughout the excavations, they found more pieces of engraved shell, a pile of six whelk shells that might be a dedicatory offering, more drilled real sharks' teeth and chert effigy ones, additional negative painted pottery with circle-and-cross motifs, exotic arrow points with Caddoan area origins and much more.

For the last few seasons, their focus was to relocate what Perino had called a "copper workshop" just off the north side of the mound and associated with a large building. They have been successful in that endeavor and have found in the soil many small fragments of sheet copper and copper dust, which often coated artifacts in that zone with a green stain. Apparently, this was an area where copper nuggets were heated and then pounded with stone hammers to form thin sheets, which were then cut into ornaments and ceremonial objects.

Their work has also led to a reevaluation of the origins of some components of the SECC, which originally was thought to have developed in the South and moved into the Cahokia area later. But with more dating of this mound and analysis of its materials, they now suggest that much of the SECC may have originated at Cahokia and moved south. This concept is being accepted by many of their colleagues and supported by other lines of evidence.

THE MOUND 44 PLAZA

This small plaza was discovered when Washington University researchers David Browman, Patty Jo Watson and Nelson Reed conducted a controlled surface collection between Merrell Mound (Mound 42) and Mound 44 to the west. The distribution of artifacts was minimal between Mound 44 and three small mounds: Mound 91 to the north, Mound 43 to the east and the proposed location of the destroyed Mound 92 to the south. This would be roughly seventy-five meters (246.0 feet) square. No excavations have taken place in this plaza or at the adjacent mounds, although in the early 1900s a scam artist sunk a metal pipe into Mound 44 hoping to convince investors that the mounds were formed by buried deposits of natural gas or something similar. It was originally a rectangular platform mound that was about five and a half meters (18.0 feet) tall, but when mapped by Fowler, it was only three meters (9.8 feet) tall, reduced by plowing like the others. When Wittry excavated Tract 15-A and the Woodhenge, just west of Mound 44, he determined that the first Woodhenge would have been superimposed by the north side of Mound 44, indicating that the mound is a later construction.

KUNNEMANN TRACT

The northernmost mound cluster considered to be part of Cahokia proper is the Kunnemann Mound Group. This cluster sits on a sand ridge that formed the north bank of the Cahokia Creek bottom north of Monks Mound. Seven mounds compose this group—Mounds 6 through 12—

although Mounds 10 and 11 are probably both part of the same mound and the largest one in the complex. Mound 6 appears to have been conical and Mound 7 a rectangular platform, and the Patrick map shows them linked by a connecting platform that is no longer apparent. Both were originally over 3.0 meters (ten feet) tall. The next mound to the west is Mound 8, an oval, flat-topped mound originally 1.5 to 2.4 meters (five to eight feet) tall. Mound 9 shows on the Patrick map having a squarish base and conical top, and it may have been 3.0 to 3.7 meters (ten to twelve feet) tall. It appears to be connected by a platform to Mound 8, but that also is no longer visible. All of these mounds have been greatly reduced in size by farming and are now just 0.6 to 1.5 meters (two to five feet) high. Originally, it was thought that none of these mounds had been excavated, but a report by Gerald Fowke in 1906 describes excavations of trenches into two of the mounds in 1905. Two burials were found near the base of one, and a variety of scattered artifacts and debris was discovered in the other, possibly unintentional inclusions in the fill used to build the mounds. Both appear to have had an initial sand core and were capped with four feet of gumbo clay. Timothy Pauketat, in his treatise on Preston Holder's excavations at Kunnemann Mound, believes that the two mounds Fowke dug into may be Mounds 8 and 9.

What Patrick labeled Mound 10 appears to be a terrace on the east side of Mound 11, and this combo is the one usually called the "Kunnemann Mound." Mound 11 may have been as tall as fifty feet or more originally, but I'll write more about that later.

Mound 12, a small conical mound remnant just to the west of Sand Prairie Lane, is the westernmost of the documented Kunnemann Mound Group, although there are a few other suspicious "bumps" farther west along the sand ridge. It appears that this is the mound where a reported cache of one hundred unfinished stone celts (axes) was found in the late 1800s. This western portion of the Kunnemann Tract is also an area where literally thousands of chert microdrills have been found by collectors and archaeologists. These small tools, some about the thickness of a wooden matchstick and from about 1.3 to 5.8 centimeters (0.5 to 1.5 inches) long, were used to drill holes in shell to make beads. They would be set in the hollow end of a narrow cane shaft that was spun with a small bow. This suggests that this was an area of craft specialization or at least a workshop area.

To get back to Mound 10/11, Moorehead, who dug there in 1921, estimated that it may have been fifteen meters (fifty feet) tall originally because as many as five meters (sixteen feet) of the top of Mound 11 reportedly had been removed around the turn of the century for fill in

Examples of marine shell beads in various stages of production and chert microdrills that were used to drill holes in the beads. *Cahokia Mounds State Historic Site.*

building a dike along Cahokia Creek. However, at least two earlier maps from the late 1800s indicate that it was nine meters (thirty feet) tall, and one from 1906 shows it as ten and a half meters (thirty-five feet) tall. It is possible that some of these maps are in error, but at least four meters (thirteen feet) of the top were removed. Portions of the west and north sides also are known to have been borrowed by contractors at different times in the past, probably reducing the length of Mound 11 by about one hundred feet. Today, it is about seven and a half meters (twenty-five feet) tall.

Moorehead trenched into the mound on the north side and observed several major stratigraphic layers above the original sand surface, each distinguished by color and texture, from "dark earth" to "yellowish loam." He also noted a couple of thin, dark "vegetation layers" between some soil zones, but state geologist Morris Leighton described these as "dark sandy silt" and "black, soil-like material." The highest zone was a dark gumbo clay. In one yellowish loam zone, a burned floor and a prepared hearth with a raised lip were found, probably associated with a former ceremonial structure.

In the mid-1950s, the Illinois State Highway Department had plans to use the soil from Mound 11 to raise the level of Sand Prairie Lane for a bridge replacement across Cahokia Canal. Preston Holder, from Washington University–St. Louis, received permission from Thorne Deuel, the Illinois state archaeologist, to conduct salvage excavations on Kunnemann Mound in 1955. Holder actually spent two seasons working on the mound, putting test trenches into all four sides, including the Mound 10 terrace. An excellent summary and analysis of Holder's work was published by Timothy Pauketat in his *Temples for Cahokia Lords*. Holder revealed numerous building stages and platforms that supported large buildings (he exposed all or parts of seventeen structures just in the areas he excavated), some of which had burned (or were burned intentionally)—some rectangular, others circular. Most had prepared puddled clay hearths in them that showed evidence of being cleaned and relined several times, probably in renewal rituals. Some structures had painted or plastered floors in black, red, yellow or white. These were likely elite-associated sacred structures or temples, as most had clean floors and little domestic debris. It is probable that several coexisted on some building stages.

Holder also found good evidence of craft activities in the pre-mound domestic zone, such as shell and woodworking tools and residue, as well as a large structure that was probably the residence of a Cahokia elite. The distribution of artifacts recovered during a controlled surface collection of the area north of the mound group at Kunnemann by SIUE archaeologists suggests that there was a residential component along most of the sandy ridge area and to the north of the main mound cluster, primarily dating to the Emergent Mississippian and early Mississippian phases. They also recovered many microdrills and other artifacts related to shell bead manufacturing.

Rattlesnake/Harding Mound/Mound 66

What was probably the second largest mound at Cahokia (it is longer than, but not as tall as, Powell Mound) was what was originally called Harding Mound, or Mound 66. It is the southernmost mound of the Cahokia group and is a ridgetop mound that was originally about 7.6 meters (25 feet) to 9.1 meters (30 feet) tall. It is oriented east to west and is approximately 132.0 meters (433 feet) long and 51.0 meters (167 feet) wide. A smaller nearby mound (Mound 64) northeast of Mound 66 was the one originally called "Rattlesnake" Mound, due not to its shape but to the presence of many of those pit vipers on and around it. In the 1930s, a U.S. Geological Survey map of the region transferred that name to Mound 66, and it has usually been referred to as Rattlesnake Mound since that time.

Warren K. Moorehead's 1927 excavations in Mound 66 (Harding/Rattlesnake Mound). He used whitewash on the soil profile to accentuate different soil horizons for the photographs. *Illinois State Museum.*

In 1927, Moorehead came back to Cahokia and did soil augering and excavations on Mound 66. He excavated a large north–south trench through the mound toward the western third, using horse-drawn slips. This revealed that it was mostly made of the local gumbo, and may have had a couple of building stages, but was probably erected fairly rapidly. About 140 burials were revealed, very poorly preserved. Most appeared to be bundle burials, and one had a chunkey stone associated with it. It is interesting that Mound 66 also occurs along the centerline proposed by Fowler, along with two smaller ridgetop mounds, Mound 72 and Mound 49, to the north. At least two smaller mounds (82 and 83) were reported to the west of Mound 66 but are no longer visible. Some aerial photographs of the area around Mound 66 suggest that there could have been some additional smaller mounds around it. There is a relatively large mound (65) to the east that is over six meters (twenty feet) tall. It was probably a rectangular platform mound but was rounded off by plowing and other disturbances. Moorehead did some testing in this mound, putting in at least forty-four auger holes to examine the stratigraphy. It had a variety of clay and sand zones in its fill and was capped with a thick layer of black gumbo clay.

Some aerial photos show what has been called a "causeway" leading north from the center of Mound 66. This was visible in relief as well and was noted by Moorehead. This causeway can still be seen in low relief north of the railroad tracks, progressing through the wooded area toward the Twin Mounds. It appears to split near there. In 1968, a test trench was dug into this causeway just south of Fox Mound (Mound 60), and Mississippian artifacts were found, as was a railroad spike. This tends to support the rumor that the railroad company had planned to mine the Twin Mounds for fill and put a rail spur in that direction. Fortunately, that did not come to fruition. It is possible that the rail spur was placed on a preexisting causeway that the Mississippians had built to traverse the low, wet terrain in that area. It may have been the primary southern approach to central Cahokia.

Today, we have problems with ATVs running over and around this mound. Although the rutting is not as serious as on some other remote mounds, it is a concern and is being monitored.

POWELL MOUND GROUP

At the western edge of the Cahokia site was a large ridgetop mound called the Powell Mound (Mound 86) after the farming family that owned it. It was oriented east to west and was ninety-four meters (310 feet) long, fifty-two meters (170 feet) wide and nine to twelve meters (30 to 40 feet) tall. Unfortunately, this mound was steam shoveled away by the owners in the winter of 1930–31. The Powells wanted to use the soil from the mound to fill a low area nearby (perhaps the borrow pit used to build the mound). They had tried to negotiate with archaeologists to excavate it, offering $3,000 and three years' time if the back dirt would be used to fill the depression, but this was deemed too big a project for most archaeologists at the time. The state did offer to buy the mound and an access road, but the family did not want to have a mushroom-shaped section taken out of their field. They did offer to sell the whole property, but the state was not interested in that.

Fearing that eminent domain was in progress, the Powells decided to go ahead with the removal of the mound. It was eight days before others were aware of the destruction in progress, and then A.R. Kelly from the University of Illinois came down to observe. Kelly was later joined by Thorne Deuel of UI and others, who conducted excavations into the basal remnant of the mound. They identified that the original mound was a platform mound about 8.3 meters (twenty-seven feet) high. The upper zone encasing this core mound formed the ridgetop shape. Before it was added, there were several burial deposits made on the platform surface. The steam shovel had destroyed one

The Powell Mound was a large ridgetop mound that marked the western boundary of what is considered Cahokia proper. Unfortunately, it was destroyed in 1931. *Paul Titterington photo, Cahokia Mounds State Historic Site.*

area, but another consisted of bundle burials placed between sheets of cedar bark and covered by blankets of marine shell beads, mostly the small *marginella* variety. All of this was covered with matting of grass or cornhusks.

In the late 1960s and 1970s, Charles Bareis conducted UI field schools at the Powell Tract when a discount store was constructed that would affect the remnant of the Powell Mound. He also tested some smaller mounds at that location and several areas of the surrounding village occupation. He believes that about two feet of some of the northern portion of the mound base is still intact on the tract, but the smaller mounds were totally destroyed by the parking lot for the store. Recently, the Archaeological Conservancy purchased the part of the Powell Tract that was not developed, and this area may include a portion of the remnant of the Powell Mound.

INTERPRETIVE CENTER TRACT

When funding was finally released in 1984 for the construction of a new Interpretive Center for Cahokia, a location had to be selected. Previous attempts at getting a new center in the 1970s failed for various reasons, although one location—the Dunham Tract just south of Woodhenge—was tested by Elizabeth Benchley of UWM and Robert Hall of the University of Illinois–Chicago Circle. Benchley did phosphate testing of the southern part of that tract, and Hall conducted magnetic tests and dug some test units. The results suggested that the archaeology would be too complex, and they recommended going elsewhere to build the museum. However, the funding eventually disappeared.

In the early 1980s, funding for testing a new location was approved, and Melvin Fowler and Elizabeth Benchley (the field director) from UWM conducted a controlled surface collection of a tract of land south of the Mounds Subdivision located south of Monks Mound. They followed this with some test units and some backhoe trenches to search for archaeological features, possible ridged fields and any buried surfaces. They did not find too many features, and the backhoe trenches revealed two buried surfaces that were utilized during Late Archaic times.

The following year, Michael Nassaney from Southern Illinois University–Carbondale conducted more extensive testing in the Interpretive Center Tract. Archaeologists confirmed the buried Archaic horizons and revealed a limited number of Mississippian-period features. The decision was made to approve this location for construction. However, for the next couple of years this field was flooded, so a decision was made to move north into the south end of the subdivision area, which was a few feet higher.

From 1984 to 1986, SIUE crews under Bill Woods did surveys and excavations in the new area, labeled Interpretive Center Tract–II (ICT-II). The difference in elevation also resulted in a dramatic increase in archaeological features. Some eighty houses and hundreds of other features were excavated, and three unrecorded mounds were identified and tested. With careful analysis of all the features, they developed a good example of how one of Cahokia's neighborhoods evolved over a two-hundred-year period, from the Lohmann to Moorehead phases. No Emergent Mississippian features were found. The community plan started with Lohmann-phase houses aligned mostly in a linear pattern running north to south and the houses aligned in the cardinal directions. Through subsequent phases, there were progressively fewer houses, but they were in clusters

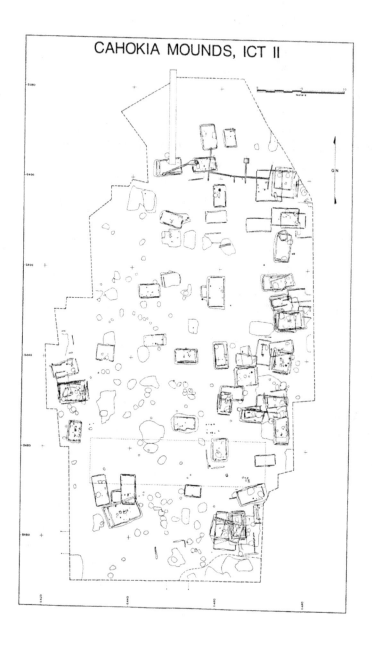

A map of the houses, pits and other features on the Interpretive Center–II Tract excavated by Southern Illinois University–Edwardsville. Analyses showed how one of Cahokia's neighborhoods evolved over time. *Illinois Historic Preservation Agency.*

116

oriented more around courtyards with less concern for cardinal alignments. House floors initially were fairly deep and the rectangular houses small, but through time the house basins became shallower and the houses larger. The final Moorehead phase had the fewest and the largest houses, but they were more square shaped. There was also a shift through time from shared storage buildings to internal storage pits in houses, perhaps as resources were becoming scarcer and there was less sharing and more hoarding.

THE TIPPETS MOUND GROUP

Southeast of the Interpretive Center is the Tippets Mound Group, with Mounds 61, 62 and 95 arranged around an irregularly shaped borrow pit. Mound 61 is a platform mound, 62 is a conical mound and 95 could be conical or ridgetop, but former historic structures on and around it have altered its form. On the 1876 Patrick map, an arcing causeway is depicted connecting Mounds 61 and 62 on the west side. It does not show on later maps, and a hedgerow in that area obscures most of where it had been. However, a very slight elevation can sometimes be seen when the field west of the hedgerow has standing water in it. Projecting northeast from Mound 62 is another straight causeway that extends into the borrow pit, and the end of the causeway expands to form a square platform, which is surrounded on three sides by water when the borrow pit is flooded.

SIUE crews did testing in the Tippets Group, including some excavation units in the square platform, which is the geometric central point from these three mounds, and they were hoping to find a post or other feature at that point. They did not find a feature there, but the results indicated that this was not an artificially built platform; rather, it may have been trimmed by the Mississippians to form the square shape. It is possible that rituals associated with these mounds took place on this peninsula out in the water.

Moorehead did do some test pits and augering in Mound 61 but found that it was basically black gumbo clay soil, and almost no artifacts were recovered. Although Patrick had mapped it as a north–south rectangular platform, Moorehead noted that it was more of an east–west oval platform. Mound 62 apparently had no testing done on it. However, the east–west base line for the equilateral triangle that Fowler drew on some of his alignment maps connected Mound 62 to Mound 68 to the west. Equal

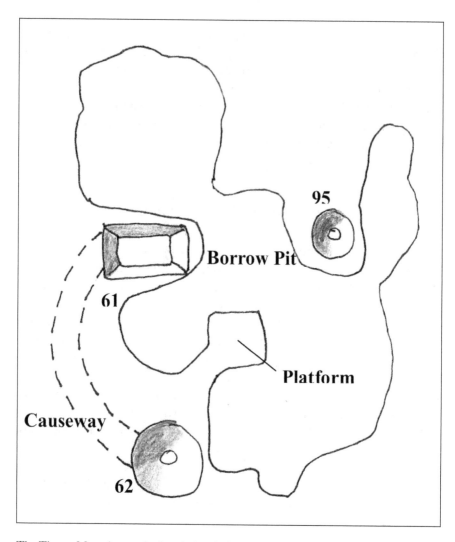

The Tippets Mound group had conical and platform "twin" mounds built around a borrow pit, with a possible connecting causeway and a ritual platform extending into the borrow pit. *William R. Iseminger, Cahokia Mounds State Historic Site.*

length lines drawn north from these two mounds converged to form the top of the triangle on the southwest corner of Monks Mound. Fowler's north–south centerline was created by bisecting that triangle.

Mound 95 is one of several "promontory" mounds found throughout the site, usually as small mounds extending on short peninsulas out into borrow pits. Like the others, the function of Mound 95 is unknown, and the historic disturbance and structures had an impact on this mound and its shape.

Small test units in the fields around these mounds showed little residential debris south of the borrow pit and increasing amounts of material as one progressed north from the borrow pit toward the central part of the site.

THE ROUCH MOUND GROUP

At the southwestern limits of the Cahokia site is an isolated group of three mounds forming the Rouch Group. The largest mound is a large rectangular platform mound, Mound 70, which was originally about twelve meters (forty feet) tall. Despite its height, it was cultivated and today is about nine meters (thirty feet) tall. There are no known excavations here. Unfortunately, it has become heavily overgrown with trees and brush and has severe erosion problems where ATVs have created paths up the sides. SIUE conducted testing and mapping at the group and located a borrow pit just north of Mound 70. Crews found that two smaller mounds—Mound 69 to the north and Mound 71 to the west—were connected to the main Mound 70 by causeways. These smaller mounds today are only small bumps in the terrain, heavily impacted by farming.

THE EAST GROUP

Mounds 1 and 2 mark the eastern limits of the Cahokia site, and they sit on the southern bank of Canteen Creek. Mound 2 appears to have been a small ridgetop mound on some early maps but later had a house built on top of it that burned recently and has been removed. Mound 1, a platform mound, also had a house on it that burned down. Gayle Fritz, John Kelly and I co-directed excavations there in 1991 to see if this was really a mound. Test trenches revealed several stages of modern soil deposits associated with earlier house construction, but beneath these the original mound was relatively intact. Its base was buried under many layers of silt from overbank flooding of Canteen Creek. Situated at this location, it is possible that this may have been a control point for access to Cahokia, as visitors from the east would have had to cross the creek, perhaps on some type of log bridge, to enter central Cahokia.

Another grouping of mounds to the west of Mounds 1 and 2 does not show up on early maps but first appears on the 1931 USGS map. Fowler included them in his atlas, but there was some question about them. These are Mounds 97 through 104. Later, John Kelly discovered a map and a reference to there having been a par-three golf course at that location, first established in the early 1930s. Thus, some of these may have been artificially constructed at that time for tees or greens. Whether preexisting small mounds were utilized or modified is not clear.

Due to space limitations, I will not go into some of the other mounds and research projects but will again refer you to the bibliography at the end of this book for sources that will provide more detailed information.

The Intriguing Woodhenges

One dark morning several years ago, I was startled out of my sleep by the pounding rhythm of "My Sharona" by The Knack on my clock radio. It was the morning of the spring equinox, and I had to get ready to head down to the reconstructed Woodhenge at Cahokia to give a presentation about Woodhenge to the usual gathering of "sun-watchers." I would talk about how it was discovered, how it works and the culture that built it. As I drove over the Collinsville bluffs toward Cahokia, the sky was an unusual dark purple color, and the full moon was preparing to set in the west over St. Louis. As I approached the Cahokia site, wispy mist hung at ground level and the mounds emerged through it. I remember thinking that I hoped the moon would not be fully set before the sun rose, as that would be an impressive sight: the opposition of the sun and moon, male and female, day and night, east and west, the underworld and the upperworld. I realized I was thinking about basic concepts of the Mississippian world. I also wondered how their leaders and priests would have explained such phenomena to the populace.

As I arrived at the Woodhenge, the parking lot was full, and cars were lined on the shoulder of Collinsville Road. Close to one hundred people were gathered by the central observation post, looking to the east as the sky began to lighten and the silhouette of Monks Mound broke the horizon. I aligned myself with the center post and the easternmost post of the 125-meter (410-foot) diameter circle of forty-eight posts and climbed my stepladder to address the group. I began my explanation as I have done since 1985, when we reconstructed this Woodhenge. As the sun eventually made its appearance, it emerged from the front of Monks Mound, near the top of the front slope. To me, this is more than coincidence, as I believe that the paramount chief was probably thought to be associated with the sun, perhaps representing the sun on earth, and to have the sun emerging from his mound would reinforce that connection and his power and authority. He may have even stood at the front of the summit to greet his "sky brother" and show him the path to take across the sky, as was recorded by the French of the Great Sun, leader of the Natchez Indians in Mississippi during the 1700s.

We don't conduct any rituals or ceremonies, as we believe this would be disrespectful to American Indians of the past and present, and since we are not of Indian heritage, we feel such activities would be inappropriate. We occasionally do get a few New Agers and "crystal people," complete with flowing robes and staffs, beating their drums and singing their chants as their minions gather about them at Woodhenge or on top of Monks Mound, but we do not encourage or sanction such activity.

DISCOVERING WOODHENGE

What do we know about Woodhenge? It must be pointed out that we did not know there was such a structure at Cahokia—it was basically discovered by accident. In the early 1960s, construction of Interstate 55/70 was in progress just north of the Woodhenge site, traversing the former Cahokia Creek bottom (the creek had been rerouted and straightened out about 1916 into a drainage canal). At that time, there was a plan for an outer-belt interstate around the Illinois side of the St. Louis metropolitan area, designated Interstate 255, to connect with I-55/70. A series of ramps and overpasses would be constructed over Collinsville Road (at that time also U.S. 40), which would impact an area of the Cahokia site designated Tract 15-A by the Illinois Department of Transportation. The Illinois State Museum had the responsibility of doing the salvage work on Tract 15-A, and Dr. Warren Wittry was put in charge of the project. He hired several young archaeologists as field supervisors and a number of local laborers to conduct the testing of the tract in 1960–61. Heavy machinery was used to peel off the disturbed plow zone in long strips across the site, and the workers then identified archaeological features, including hundreds of houses, storage and refuse pits and lots of large post pits. As the excavations expanded into more of the area, additional features were exposed, showing that it had experienced intense occupation. There were basically two types of rectangular houses encountered—Emergent Mississippian posthole structures and Mississippian wall trench structures, often with the latter superimposing the former, indicating the sequence of occupation.

Wittry was intrigued by the number of large post pits they discovered. He often referred to them as "bathtubs" to describe their shape, which resembled an old-fashioned metal bathtub. Generally, these appeared as long, oval-shaped dark stains averaging about seven feet long and over two feet wide. When excavated, they turned out to be just over 1.2 meters (four feet) deep at one end, with a ramp extending to the surface at the other end. Some post pits even had what Wittry called "post prints," impressions in the soil at the bottom of the pit compressed by the butt end of the posts. The ramps were for insertion (or extraction) of the posts. It would be virtually impossible to raise a post vertically, slide it over and insert it into a cylindrical round hole because of the great weight and size (we estimate they were 6.0 meters [twenty feet] tall above ground and forty-six to sixty-one centimeters [eighteen to twenty-four inches] in diameter), so the posts were slid down the ramps and then pulled upright with ropes, and the soil was packed in around them.

Wittry decided to make a separate map of the large post pits to see if there was any pattern to them, and when he did, he realized that many of them were forming arcs or circles. At that time, he identified four possible circles. Some only had three to six posts identified, but the arcs they formed were enough to determine the diameters of the circles they represented, ranging from 73 meters (240 feet) to nearly 146 meters (480 feet). It was then that he began referring to them as the "American Woodhenge," as he believed they were used to track the movements of the sun. His colleague, Dr. Robert Hall, continued the exploration of the Woodhenge in 1963, pursuing the arcs to see if more post pits could be located. This goal he successfully achieved, finding several more. He also dug near the centers of the circles and located some larger post pits that appear to be the central observation posts. When he and Wittry put all of this information together, they could see that the circle for which they had the most posts revealed, Circle 2, had its centerpost offset to the east from the geometric center of the circle about 1.7 meters (5.6 feet). This provided a slightly wider angle to properly align with the perimeter posts that mark the summer and winter solstices at this latitude. This correction factor helped to confirm the function of this post-circle monument as a solar calendar.

Construction of one of the Woodhenges with Mounds 44 and 42 and Monks Mound in the distance. *Lloyd K. Townsend, Cahokia Mounds State Historic Site.*

Pre-Woodhenge structures at Tract 15-A—two Mississippian wall trench structures superimposed over an Emergent Mississippian posthole structure. *Illinois State Museum.*

Fortunately, the I-255 project was put on hold, and when it was reactivated later, with stronger federal preservation laws now in effect, it was moved about three miles to the east and renamed the FAI-270 project, even though the highway was eventually designated I-255. However, Tract 15-A became a dumping ground for IDOT, with lots of rubble being deposited there over the years, though most of this was cleaned up to some extent when the tract was transferred to our agency.

Wittry returned in 1977–78 to continue Woodhenge excavations, especially for Circle 2, since that was the one he had the most posts for thus far, and he wanted to excavate one circle as completely as possible. He was able to locate most of the remaining post positions, except for nine on the western side that had been destroyed by a highway borrow pit before Woodhenge was discovered and three in the northeastern sector.

Dr. Warren Wittry examining one of the Woodhenge post pits with its long insertion ramp. *Illinois State Museum.*

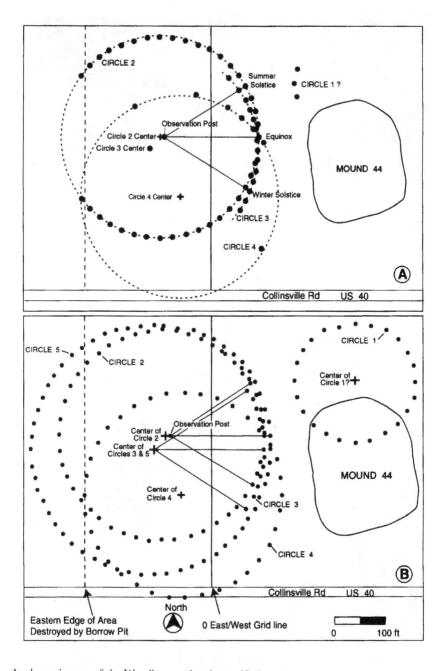

A schematic map of the Woodhenges showing verified post locations based on excavations (upper) and projected complete circles based on the spacing between known posts (bottom). Only the third Woodhenge has been extensively excavated. *Wisconsin Archaeologist, 1996.*

During those excavations, he found a slab of red cedar in one of the post pits and more fragments in some others. The slab was a remnant of one of the posts that apparently broke off when being removed, perhaps in a repair project or when a subsequent Woodhenge was being built. It seems significant that the Cahokians were using red cedar for the posts, as that wood is often considered sacred by many Indian groups. In our area, it is the only native evergreen tree, remaining green year-round, and it has reddish heartwood. These are symbolic of life and blood, which were factors that made it sacred. Cedar also resists insects and decay. Additionally, Wittry noticed that in the soil around some of the post pits there was some red ochre, a claylike iron ore that was often used to make a red pigment or paint, and he speculated that the posts may have been painted red or had some red designs painted on them. Red ochre is also symbolic of blood and life for many Indian peoples.

At the end of the 1978 season, Wittry had utility poles placed at the central post position and those of the equinox and solstices, standing about nine meters (thirty feet) above ground, so that he could test the hypothesis that these would align with the sun on those dates. In September of that year, at the fall equinox, he placed a deer hunter's stand rigged to hold an array of cameras near the top of the post. He conjectured that the Mississippian sun priest may have had some type of platform at such a higher elevation in order to have a clearer view of the horizon and to be above the rooftops and walls of the city. He shakily climbed a ladder to get to the platform, worked his way around to the seat and positioned himself and his cameras for the sunrise. He was justly rewarded with a beautiful sunrise through a slightly hazy sky. The first limb of the red-orange sun broke past the upper slope of Monks Mound and aligned perfectly with the top of the easternmost post of the circle as a cheer erupted from the crowd that had gathered to watch the event. Wittry returned for subsequent solstice and equinox sunrises with equal success.

Wittry did get permission from the landowners of the borrow pit property that had impacted the west side of the Woodhenges to see if there were any remnants that had survived. His tests were negative, as that area had been deeply stripped, removing all evidence of those nine posts.

About this same time, Wittry was trying to determine the nature of a couple of paired posts on the northern arc of Circle 2. He toyed with the idea that they might represent the rising and setting positions of the bright star Capella, but he later abandoned that idea, realizing that these posts were part of a fifth Woodhenge that shared a center point with one of the other circles.

RECONSTRUCTING WOODHENGE

In 1985, a local couple, George and Mildred Arnold, who were fans of Cahokia and the Woodhenge, donated funds to reconstruct all of the known posts of this circle. As part of that project, I conducted a public field school for the Cahokia Mounds Museum Society at Woodhenge to find the last three posts on the northeastern segment; this goal was achieved, and we found the post pits within inches of where Wittry predicted they would be. This allowed us to be able to erect thirty-nine posts around the circumference and the central observation post. We were able to acquire only twenty cedar trees, which were cut from across the river in Missouri. The remaining posts were black locust trees that were cut locally. Volunteer Larry Kinsella spearheaded the reconstruction project with assistance from other Cahokia volunteers and members of the Cahokia Archaeological Society. Larry, who is an expert flintknapper, toolmaker and experimental archaeologist, had made stone axes in the same manner as the Cahokians, and these were used to cut the limbs off the trees so that we would have the same types of tool marks on the posts. This involved a tremendous amount of work, as cedar

Reconstruction of Woodhenge 3 at the original location. *Cahokia Mounds State Historic Site.*

trees have a plethora of limbs. We also stripped the bark from the trees and stained them with red ochre. The post pit for the center post was dug using stone hoes, and we removed the soil in baskets, as would have been done by the Cahokians. The post was then rolled to the hole and slipped down the ramp. The volunteer crew raised the post by hand and with ropes and tamped the soil around it.

On the day of the dedication ceremony, we had a program on Woodhenge and then we all drove to the reconstruction. Ironically, just as we arrived a lightning bolt from an isolated cloud struck a tree next to the Woodhenge and ricocheted to hit one of the posts. Then the sky cleared and we continued with the program. What a formal dedication from the "Upperworld"!

WOODHENGE STATISTICS

When Wittry first assigned numbers to the circles, it was not clear what the exact sequence was. With his later excavations and the realization of a fifth circle, he was able to determine the actual sequence and renamed it, this time calling them Woodhenges instead of "circles." Thus, Circle 1 remained Woodhenge 1; Circle 2 became Woodhenge 3; Circle 3 became Woodhenge 5; Circle 4 became Woodhenge 2; and Circle 5 became Woodhenge 4.

This revised sequence also reflects an increase (by twelve) in the number of posts with each construction:

Woodhenge 1: 240 feet (73.1 meters) in diameter, twenty-four posts
Woodhenge 2: 408 feet (124.4 meters) in diameter, thirty-six posts
Woodhenge 3: 410 feet (125 meters) in diameter, forty-eight posts
Woodhenge 4: 476 feet (145 meters) in diameter, sixty posts
Woodhenge 5: 446 feet (136 meters) in diameter, seventy-two posts (if it had been a complete circle, but only thirteen posts on the eastern arc were found)

This poses some questions: why the changing number of posts and diameters and the shifting of the center points for most of the Woodhenges? There have been suggestions that the increase of twelve posts each time might reflect a method of tracking lunar cycles or some other type of day counts. Some of this may just be a result of simple geometry when dividing a circle into equal parts, although one could have a larger circle with the same number of posts. Perhaps the Cahokians were introducing more ritual and festival dates into their calendar and needed additional posts to mark those dates, and to produce symmetry, more posts were placed around the entire circumference. The reasons for changing the diameter are not clear as there is no regularity to the change, other than to enclose a larger space. Having only the sunrise arc for the final Woodhenge is interesting. One wonders if it could be something as simple as the lack of red cedar trees of sufficient size, or perhaps there was some other cultural change occurring that resulted in a diminished usage of this as a sacred enclosure. The dating for the Woodhenges has now been established for the period from AD 1100 to AD 1200. The latter part of the century is when changes were occurring at Cahokia and elsewhere, as population began to diminish and also when the stockade was first constructed.

As for the changing center point, I have suggested that since the equinox alignment with the front of Monks Mound was important, perhaps the changing size and shape of Monks Mound over time may have necessitated moving the observation points—but that is just a guess. We are still learning more about Monks Mound with recent research, and it is believed that most of the major construction on it occurred during the same century as Woodhenge. This lends some support to my hypothesis.

Woodhenge 3 (formerly Circle 2) is the most completely excavated Woodhenge and the one we know the most about. The posts were seven degrees, thirty minutes apart as measured from the geometric center of the circle. The angle from the center post to the summer solstice post was just over thirty degrees north of east, and the winter solstice post was a little more than that south of east. Wittry was intrigued by this winter solstice offset when he first erected the utility poles in 1978. He knew that the post was in the same position as the original, but when the sun rose, it was to the left of the post; it was not until a minute or two later that the sun actually aligned with the post. Wittry got up on a ladder near the top of the center post during the daytime with his cameras to test an idea he had. He aimed to the winter solstice post position, using a telephoto lens. What he saw confirmed his suspicions—in line with the actual sunrise position was Fox Mound (Mound 60) of the Twin Mounds, and it projected slightly above the horizon. This large platform mound would have had a building on top of it, so the rising sun would have had to clear that mound and building before it could be seen from the center post. When it would first be visible was in the position of the offset solstice post. This additional "correction factor" also lends support to the function of Woodhenge as a sun calendar.

The Intriguing Woodhenges

The fall equinox sunrise at the reconstructed Woodhenge. At the equinoxes, the sun appears to emerge from the front of Monks Mound as it aligns with the center post and easternmost post. *Cahokia Mounds State Historic Site.*

The solar calendar function, marking the rising sun at the equinoxes and solstices, was important, and it is likely that there were rituals held at those events. The solstices would seem to be of greater importance—the sun reaches its northernmost point at summer solstice and southernmost rising position at winter solstice. The ritual at winter solstice would probably have been to encourage the sun to stop heading south and return for another cycle to re-warm the earth and bring back all of the essential plant and animal life the Indians depended on. Indeed, the sun does appear to halt its journey for about five days before reversing its course at the solstices.

The equinoxes occur close to planting and harvest times but would not have been used to schedule those events, since other environmental factors determined when to do that. Some later Indians would not plant until the leaves on an oak tree were as big as a squirrel's ears, or other similar natural phenomena. However, the equinoxes would be the time to hold the rituals and ceremonies to prepare for planting or harvest or to ensure a successful growing season and crop yield.

OTHER POSSIBLE FUNCTIONS FOR WOODHENGE

Undoubtedly, there were other important dates in their ritual calendar that were determined by other post and sun alignments, but the Woodhenges may have had other functions as well. Since only the eastern sunrise posts were essential (and possibly sunset positions as well), why have a full circle? There was symbolism to the circle, representing the cycles of life and the seasons. Indian peoples look at time as cyclical, whereas today we look at it from a more linear perspective. The circle also represents Earth, as seen in much of the Mississippian iconography, especially the circle and cross motif, with the cross representing the four cardinal directions, the four winds or the four quarters of the earth. The sun is also a disc or circle in the sky. The Woodhenge was an earthly embodiment of a spiritual concept.

The Woodhenge would also enclose a sacred space where some of these rituals took place. But what was important about this particular space—why here? There is no clear answer at this time. As mentioned previously, there were hundreds of houses, pits and other features that show that this area was initially a residential zone prior to the construction of the Woodhenges, as evidenced by the many Emergent Mississippian structures. Then the Woodhenges were built over a one-hundred-year period, followed by a return to residential usage of this location. Society was changing, as noted before, and this was a time of redirection at Cahokia. It is possible that a calendric structure was no longer needed or was erected elsewhere or in another form. Or perhaps some other time-tracking systems were developed.

Other researchers have suggested additional functions for Woodhenge. Clay Sherrod and Martha Rolingson of the Arkansas Archaeological Survey were examining mound sites in the lower Mississippi Valley to see if there were standard units of measure being utilized or other significant alignments, and they believed that they had good evidence to support that concept. They wondered if the same could be said for Cahokia, so they did an analysis of the Woodhenge circles, especially the alignments of the posts with mounds. With as many posts and mounds as there are, there are bound to be a number of alignments, but they did see a greater number than would be accountable simply by chance or coincidence. They thought that the Woodhenge might also have served as an engineering device to help with the layout of the city and its many mounds—what they termed the "Cahokia Aligner." However, some mound alignments would not necessarily have been visible from Woodhenge, especially those to the east, which would have been blocked by the massiveness of Monks Mound. Thus, they suggested there might

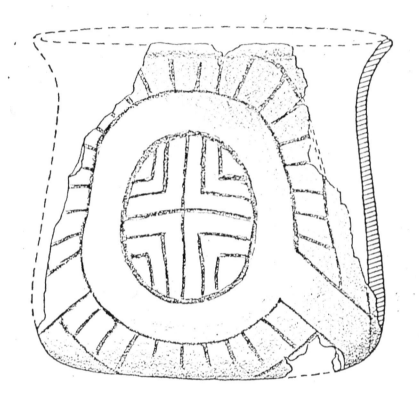

A sketch of the design on a beaker found in a pit near a winter solstice post. The design has the circle-and-cross world symbol, an exterior rayed sun circle and extending channels at positions consistent with the winter solstice sunrise and sunset if viewed as a "map" of Woodhenge. *Adapted from Illinois State Museum.*

be other "aligner" circles at strategic locations around the site to lay out the mounds in that sector or perhaps to triangulate between sectors. They suggested some locations—one being near Mound 72—which led Melvin Fowler to reexamine his excavation maps and records and the relationship between nearby Mound 96 and Mound 72 to see if he had evidence for a post circle there (as discussed in the chapter on Mound 72).

Bruce Smith, of the Smithsonian Institution, sees the Woodhenges as anchoring the entire Cahokian world view of the cosmos in their symbolic form and "legitimizing the place of the Cahokia elite in the cosmological scheme of things." These circles served as containers of esoteric knowledge under control of the elite and, as monuments under their control, confirmed the link between the chiefly elite and the sun. The elite had the power to schedule the ceremonies, which often involved the distribution of goods and services and helped integrate the members of their society, deriving that authority from the sun. This authority fell especially to the paramount chief, who may have lived on, but at least governed from, Monks Mound, the mound closest to the sun.

Others have challenged the function of Woodhenge as a calendar, and since Wittry's passing, Dr. Michael Friedlander, a physicist at Washington University in St. Louis, has taken Wittry's data and reexamined it. He has shown that some of Wittry's detractors were using flawed data and logic in their objections. His studies have confirmed what Wittry presented.

Defending Cahokia

The Stockade/Palisade

STOCKADE FUNCTION

Sometime late in the 1100s, the Cahokians fortified the center of their city
with a log wall nearly two miles long, enclosing Monks Mound, the Grand
Plaza and at least seventeen other mounds in what has been called the
"Central Ceremonial Precinct," an area of sixty to eighty hectares (150 to
200 acres). This "stockade," or "palisade" (the terms are interchangeable),
was primarily a defensive feature as indicated by the regularly spaced
bastions, or guard towers, that projected out from the wall. From raised
platforms in these bastions, warriors could launch arrows against attackers
and protect the face of the wall, controlling access through the L-shaped
entryways between some of the bastions. Nearly thirty years of investigation
have revealed information about not only the form of the defensive system
but also the culture that produced it and the impact it had on the society and
the environment.

It is not clear who the "enemy" was, but it almost had to be other
Mississippians. Whether they were from distant areas and occasionally
raided the Cahokia area or whether they were from some of the more local
Mississippian communities that may have challenged Cahokia's authority is
not clear. However, the threat of attack—real or perceived—was continuous
since the stockade was built at least four times. There is no direct evidence
for wall destruction in the excavated areas, and it is proposed that a new

A reconstruction of the second stockade and its bastions in the original location, with Monks Mound in the background. The left end has a simulation of daub plastering. *Cahokia Mounds State Historic Site.*

wall was constructed to replace one weakened by decay and age. Occasional "extraction pits" have been noted, indicating repairs to a standing wall, but these are usually limited to single posts that probably decayed at a faster rate than those adjacent to them. Ceramic data and radiocarbon dates indicate that construction of all four stockades occurred during the Late Stirling and Moorehead phases and most likely over the one-hundred-year period from about AD 1175 to 1275. This is the period when there was a lot of political change occurring—Cahokia's population was diminishing, and evidence for conflict and warfare was increasing. These changes were happening not just at Cahokia but also throughout the Mississippian world, as communities large and small were being fortified.

In Cahokia society, the stockade also must have served a social function. Since the city continued for one mile outside the wall where most of the mounds and extensive habitation areas were located, there must have been some difference between those who lived within the walled district and those who resided outside. Although there have been few excavations of residential units within the walled precinct, it is assumed that those living there were probably Cahokia's elite. However, there were many elite areas outside the central precinct as well, but we don't know how or why they were different from those living within. Perhaps those belonging to certain kin groups were privileged or were related to the paramount chief in some way. It is possible that access was limited to those residing there and those who had business with them—though, of course, access would be granted to the general population on certain dates for public gatherings, festivals, rituals, markets and other special occasions. Presumably, public access would also have been required whenever defense against external forces was necessary.

STOCKADE FORM

The stockade was first discovered at Cahokia in 1966. Prior to that, Dr. Melvin Fowler of the University of Wisconsin–Milwaukee had a National Science Foundation grant for the Cahokia Mapping Project. The primary purpose was to create a modern, accurate map of the site, as the former most accurate one had been commissioned about 1876 by Dr. J.R.R. Patrick. As a result, a photogrammetic contour map of the whole site was produced that included the existing mounds in the mid-1960s, as well as modern structures, highways, etc. Another part of the project was to gather all known maps, illustrations and photographs of the Cahokia site. It was several sets of early aerial photographs that revealed soil discolorations in plowed fields where the stockade had been built several times. These included what are believed to be the first aerial photos of an American archaeological site, made in 1922 by Lieutenants Ramey and Goddard. They took oblique angled photos of the mounds and surrounding terrain. In the dark, plowed fields east of Monks Mound, a light, linear soil stain was observed progressing south and curving southwest to the area of the Twin Mounds. However, a similar line was not clearly visible west of the Grand Plaza or Monks Mound. Later, in 1933, Daesche Reeves took a series of vertical aerial photographs of the site, and the linear soil stains were still visible in these images. There were also suggestions of some lines just west of the Twin Mounds and possibly to the northwest of Monks Mound.

Scaling off the location of these lines east of Monks Mound onto the Cahokia Map, Fowler's crew, led by Jim Anderson, began excavation in 1966 and 1967. At that time, they identified at least three stockade trenches once they got below the plow zone. They also realized they were in an intensively occupied part of the site, with numerous house basins, refuse and storage pits and many other residential features, often superimposed on one another. Many of these features were truncated by the various stockade trenches, which ranged from 1.0 to 1.5 meters (3.3 to 5.0 feet) deep, indicating the sequence of activities at the site and how the usage of certain parts of the site changed through time—another example of urban renewal.

The first stockade had small round bastions, the second had large square ones and the third and fourth had progressively smaller open-backed rectangular ones. The reduction in size may reflect dwindling tree resources and an attempt to conserve on how many were being used, and they probably reused as many as possible with each construction. Screened gates have been identified in association with the second and third stockades along the East Stockade. These L-shaped walls extend out from the curtain wall from 0.8 to 1.8 meters (averaging about 1.5 meters or 5.0 feet) and then turn south for 2.7 to 4.5 meters (averaging about 3.5 meters or 11.5 feet). The narrow opening faces the adjacent bastion, making them easily defensible. Although no gates have been firmly identified with Stockades 1 or 4 in the excavated areas, it is assumed that they would be of similar form but would occur beyond those areas exposed by excavation or perhaps at a less frequent interval.

Although there is no conclusive evidence for a daub-plastered stockade, covering the wall with a thick layer of daub—a mixture of clay and chopped grass—would certainly have extended the survival rate of a wall, serving as protection from weather and fire. Daub associated with stockade walls has been found at Aztalan in Wisconsin and at Angel Mounds in Indiana, and daubed walls are well documented for latter-day Mississippian sites encountered by the DeSoto entrada in the Southeast (see Varner and Varner, 1951). Thus, it is not unlikely that Cahokia's stockade was plastered, but unless a section was hardened by fire, as at Aztalan, the daub would not survive the centuries of weathering and cultivation. Only small fragments of daub (usually burned) were found during East Stockade excavations, and these could well have been associated with houses or other structures. During the Cahokia Interpretive Center Tract excavations, it was noted by Jim Collins that the "unfired mud or daub walls of some ICT-II structures… probably disintegrated in the tract's extremely wet, acid environment. This would account for the general absence of daub from excavated features." A study by McIntosh of mud wall decay of West African structures found that in wet environments "the persistent humidity and acidity of the local soils breaks down buried wall material." Such conditions certainly describe most of the Cahokia site and could explain the absence of daub associated with the stockades. Perhaps the visibility of the light streaks in the farmers' fields is partly due to deposition of "melted" daub along the stockade route.

The East Stockade excavations of a square bastion from Stockade 2, superimposing a circular bastion from Stockade 1 and several pre-stockade storage and refuse pits. All four stockades were built in about the same alignment. *Richard Norrish photo, Cahokia Mounds State Historic Site.*

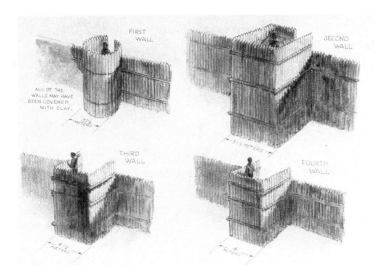

An illustration of the four bastion types that identify the sequence of construction. *George Bloodsworth, Cahokia Mounds State Historic Site.*

Still, after a period of time a wall had to be replaced, as insects and moisture ravaged the portions of the posts embedded in the ground. We experienced this in the late 1970s when we built a stockade enclosure around the backside of the old museum to protect experimental houses and a garden. We used trees cut from the large borrow pit at Cahokia, which were mostly bottomland softwoods. We did not remove the bark from the trees, and we soon learned how important that step was. The portions above ground soon were riddled with boring insects that favored the environment just under the bark, and within a couple years, the portions in the ground were heavily decayed and began falling over.

Following the construction of an Emergent Mississippian pit house by Errett Callahan, we decided to replace that stockade with a new, more secure one. Larry Kinsella took on the project and utilized replicated stone tools to do most of the work in the mid-1980s. He acquired black locust trees from the uplands, a hardwood that many farmers use for fence posts. He also burned the top and bottom ends of the posts to harden them and discourage insects and decay (evidence for burned post bases had been found at the Aztalan site in Wisconsin) and removed the bark. The posts were inserted into trenches, and they were still in good shape when we tore down the old museum and recycled the posts to enclose a courtyard at the new Interpretive Center in 1989. Twenty years later, most of these posts are still standing, but many now need replacement. This conforms well to the proposed one-hundred-year time span for the stockades, or about twenty-five years for each of the four walls.

THE STOCKADE ROUTE

Although other terminology occasionally has been used, the following terms define the various segments of the known and proposed stockade/palisade route, forming an asymmetrical hexagon: "East Stockade," from the former Cahokia Creek bank on the north to just east of Murdock Mound (55) to the south; "Southeast Stockade" for the section angling northeast–southwest from Murdock Mound to near Fox Mound (60); "South Stockade" for the east–west section south of the Twin Mounds (Fox Mound and Roundtop Mound); "Southwest Stockade" for the proposed segment angling southeast–northwest around Roundtop Mound (59); "West Stockade," from the point it turns north along the west side of the Grand Plaza and Mound 57 and angles around the west side of Mound 48 and the proposed location west of Mounds 41, 40, 77 and 39; and the "North Stockade," proposed to run west–east behind Monks Mound, connecting the East and West Stockade. Excavations thus far have identified portions of the East, Southeast, South and West Stockades and a small segment of the North Stockade where one wall heads west from the East Stockade.

However, some of the 1973–74 excavations on the East Stockade showed that several of the East Stockade trenches were continuing north over the south bank and into the bottomland of Cahokia Creek and then bending slightly to the northwest. Unfortunately, at that point only the very bottoms of some of the trenches or deeper posts were still visible, as erosion by Cahokia Creek over the past centuries had truncated most of the evidence. Future research may establish whether any other remnants of the trenches—particularly bastion trenches that generally are about fifty centimeters deeper than the main curtain trenches—are still extant and which of the walls they represent. It is curious that the walls were built in the creek bottom, where they were subject to excessive moisture and occasional flooding. Perhaps the intent was to include part of the creek system inside the wall to guarantee a flowing water supply. Or perhaps the wall was built during a dry period, when excess moisture was not a problem. There are at least four, and possibly five, mounds in this creek bottom area demarcating the North Plaza, and this may also suggest construction during a dry period. Evidence has been introduced recently indicating that there was an extended drought in the Midwest from AD 1135 to 1170 which supports this interpretation.

During the 1967 excavations, a small portion of one trench was exposed, emanating from a confusing array of linear and curvilinear trenches on the East Stockade and heading due west toward the backside of Monks Mound. It is possible this trench complex may represent some type of corner entryway. Since 2004, this "corner" of the wall has been the focus of continuing excavations to follow the westward track of the wall and to locate a bastion, which would identify which of the four walls it represents. It was thought to be either the first stockade, with the round bastions, or possibly the fourth stockade, with the open-backed bastions. During the 2009 field season, excavators found what appears to be part of an open-backed bastion, which indicates that it is probably the fourth wall. This suggests that as the resources needed to build the walls—primarily available trees and labor—were dwindling, the Mississippians were shrinking the area enclosed by the wall on the north side. Another possibility is that the extended drought had come to an end and the normally dry creek bottom area was once again too wet for construction.

STOCKADE LOGISTICS

The construction of any one of the walls was a massive undertaking, requiring a major labor force, a huge quantity of materials and a large expenditure of time. It is likely that corvée labor was imposed on the general population of Cahokia and members of outlying communities, who could have contributed to the project with labor and logs.

In working out the numbers and calculations that follow, average figures were utilized and rounded upward. Thus, the totals could vary above or below the numbers projected, depending on the exact route of the wall and the type and number of bastions and gates. Additionally, some figures have been revised from earlier estimates I made in 1990.

The suggested route of the stockade and its trenches is approximately 2,800 meters (1.75 miles), assuming a complete enclosure. There would be an additional 1,545 meters (5,068.0 feet) of bastion trenches, using an arbitrary figure for three sides averaging 5 meters (16.4 feet) each for 103 bastions spaced an average of 27 meters (88.5 feet) apart, center to center.

Post diameters generally ranged from twenty to forty centimeters (eight to sixteen inches), for an average post diameter of thirty centimeters, or 3.5 posts per meter if the posts butted against one another, as this would be the most efficient system for defense. For the curtain wall, 9,800 posts would be needed and 5,410 posts for the bastion walls. An additional 2,060 logs for bastion platform floors (averaging 20 each) would be required. The number or spacing of gates is unknown, but seven were noted in the northern portion of the East Stockade excavations associated with walls 2 and 3. These L-shaped walls have an average total length of about five meters. Several hundred posts would be needed for these gates. George Milner, in his discussion of some of my previous construction figures, noted that with thirty gates the palisade would "leak like a sieve." James Anderson (personal communication) suggested years ago that some of these may have been "blind gates" that had no interior opening in order to confuse and trap attackers. However many there were, one would expect there to be, minimally, several on the east, south and west sides to facilitate entry for the populace and on the north side adjacent to Cahokia Creek to provide access from the beached dugout canoes or people walking in from the north.

Thus, for the primary construction of an "average" wall, nearly eighteen thousand logs would be needed. More than likely, these were five to six meters (sixteen to twenty feet) long, if one assumes that for every foot in the ground there would be four or five feet above ground, which is also a modern rule of thumb for placing large posts.

In addition, to stabilize the posts and keep them vertical, it would be necessary to use horizontal lathes or withes. At a minimum, a parallel pair of lathes on either side of the wall, lashed together between posts, would be needed near the top. For the 4,500 meters (14,764.0 feet) of curtain, bastion and gate walls, this means some 1,800 poles would be needed if they averaged 5 meters (16.5 feet) long, probably made of saplings or young trees. If the wall was daubed, additional lathes would be needed measuring the full height of the wall, increasing manifold the number of poles required. However, in these calculations, only the minimum numbers are used.

Based on the above estimates, a total of nearly twenty thousand trees of various dimensions had to be cut. It is probable that two or more posts could be obtained from some of the taller trees, but the twenty thousand figure will be used here.

Wood specimens that can be directly attributed to the stockade construction are extremely rare, and most have been identified as oak and hickory (James P. Anderson, personal communication, per examination by Lawrence Conrad). Oaks and hickories, although occurring in the flood plain, were significantly more abundant along the bluff slopes and uplands along the eastern perimeter of the American Bottom, beginning three to five kilometers (two to five miles) from the Cahokia site. Other species may have been used, but preference would have been given to straight-growing trees with a primary trunk and smaller limbs.

Although Neil Lopinot estimates that the total number of trees in a ten-kilometer (six-mile) catchment centered on Monks Mound would be 628,000, based on data derived from the early 1800s Government Land Office (GLO) records, not all species would be suitable for stockade construction. White oaks, primarily an upland species, have very rot-resistant heartwood and would seem to be a preferable construction material. It was a dominant species recovered from the Cahokia Interpretive Center Tract excavations, although mostly as charcoal fragments, and presumably was used for both construction and fuel.

Whatever the source of the timber, a tremendous amount of labor was needed to chop it down, remove the limbs and bark and transport it to Cahokia—four times. Just as Monks Mound was the largest earth-moving project, the stockades were the largest public construction projects at Cahokia. All of this was probably done by groups of laborers performing these tasks as crews working under the supervision of leaders

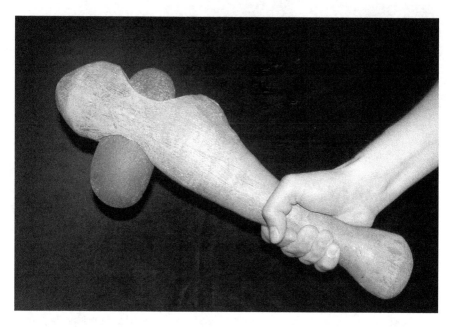

Trees were cut down with ground stone axes made of diorite or basalt and hafted in a wooden handle. *Cahokia Mounds State Historic Site.*

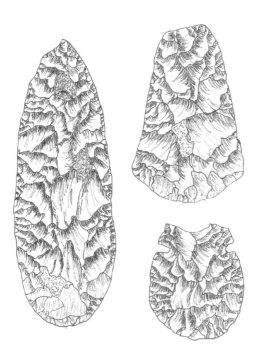

Stockade trenches and other digging projects were done with three types of hoes made from Mill Creek chert from southern Illinois and lashed with rawhide to L-shaped handles. *William R. Iseminger, Cahokia Mounds State Historic Site.*

and supervisors, and all of it would certainly have been under the direction of the paramount chief and his minions. A side benefit of cutting down so many trees would be the generation of tremendous amounts of firewood, a commodity in great demand in a community the size of Cahokia, with all its cooking and heating fires. Most likely, the majority of the firewood would have been collected and transported by the women and children, while the transportation of the logs would have been a male-oriented task.

Getting the timber to Cahokia would also have been a major task. It had to be dragged or carried by teams of workers over the total distance to the site or by floating it part of the way along nearby streams such as Canteen and Cahokia Creeks. Once it arrived at the site, it had to be inserted into the deep trenches. The trenches were dug with stone hoes made from Mill Creek chert, which outcrops in tabular form in southern Illinois near the town of that name, and some were over a foot long. Tied to an L-shaped handle with rawhide lashings, they were used much like a hoe or pick of today to dig the deep trenches for the posts. Much of the route of the southern half of the stockade was through dense clay soils, which is challenging to dig even with modern sharpened-steel tools. The northern half of the route is more of a silty soil, along a wide, slightly elevated ridge that formed as a natural levee from a very old, abandoned channel of the Mississippi known as the Edelhardt Meander Scar.

The construction of the stockades may have contributed to Cahokia's decline, as cutting so many trees in addition to those already being cut for other construction projects over a couple hundred years would have had an impact on the local forests, where various flora and fauna that were important to the Cahokians thrived. It is important to remember that Cahokia was not alone in this region and that there were many other large and small communities also depending on the forest resources. As these resources became scarcer, competition for what was left increased. This would also have increased the incidents of threat or conflict and thus created a greater need for defensive structures such as the stockades. Bill Woods and Neal Lopinot have suggested that cutting so many trees from the bluff slopes and bluffs resulted in more runoff and erosion, leading to siltation of the bottomland streams. In turn, this increased the amount of localized flooding of bottomland fields during storm conditions. The extent of this impact is speculative and would probably have been limited to the areas immediately around the streams involved, but when coupled with drought conditions and other sociopolitical problems in the Cahokia world, it could have been one more factor leading to Cahokia's demise.

The Demise of Cahokia

We know that by the mid-1300s Cahokia was basically abandoned, but what happened to cause the decline and demise of this once great Indian city? There are many factors that probably played a role, and it probably was not just one, but a combination of them all, that brought about Cahokia's downfall. Resource depletion, environmental degradation, political turmoil, warfare, disease and crop failure are some of the causes that have been considered, but many of these are not mutually exclusive. It is likely that they all worked together, leading to the eventual abandonment of Cahokia.

The first signs of change at Cahokia, following its peak period of development during the Stirling phase, occur during the Late Stirling and early Moorehead phases. At that time, we see the construction of the first stockade around central Cahokia around AD 1175 and the sealing of the top of Monks Mound after the large building was removed. Activities then seemed to shift to the First Terrace. Also, about AD 1200, the Woodhenge apparently was dismantled and that area was returned to residential use. The area of the compounds on Tract 15-B also reverted to residential structures. A number of smaller mounds were built, especially in the areas to the east of the Grand Plaza and stockade, and mantles of soil were added to existing mounds. Excavations at the Interpretive Center Tract and other tracts indicate there were progressively fewer houses erected.

All of this seems to represent a lateral shift at Cahokia, perhaps changing from a major population center to one that was focused more on ritual activity and a shrinking residential area, although it was still the biggest

The Demise of Cahokia

The size of Cahokia and the number of subordinate communities stressed the resources and political structure needed to support the system. *Middie Schmidt, Cahokia Mounds State Historic Site.*

thing around. Eventually, Cahokia collapsed under its own weight. It had become a lumbering giant that was no longer able to support itself, and the once subordinate communities it ruled had become more autonomous and less dependent on Cahokia, perhaps even challenging Cahokia's authority. The population began to gradually disperse, some going into the nearby hinterlands to establish new communities or joining those where they had kinfolk and others migrating longer distances, primarily to the north, adapting to those areas and bringing a little bit of Cahokia with them, as is reflected in their pottery, tools and iconography.

RESOURCE DEPLETION

Regardless of what population figures one uses for Cahokia and the surrounding region, the impact of thousands of people over hundreds of years would have had a deleterious effect on the local ecology. The amount of timber needed for construction of houses, temples, stockades and firewood was massive, and after a period of time there probably were few trees standing in the bottomlands other than scrub growth. Cutting the forests would have impacted the habitats of plants and animals that were important to the Mississippians. It has also been suggested that overcutting the bluffs and bluff slopes to the east would have led to increased erosion and resulting siltation of bottomland streams, which would have flooded local agricultural fields during storm events.

Excavation at the Interpretive Center Tract showed that there was selection of preferred woods for building houses in the early phases of occupation, but in later phases, whatever was available was being used. As resources became scarcer, the Cahokians would have had to travel farther out to obtain what they needed, resulting in territorial conflicts and possibly raids. The amount of deer, fish and fowl needed would have dwindled as their numbers and habitats were reduced.

It is not known if the Mississippians rotated crops as we do today, and we have no evidence that they used fertilizer. Throughout the centuries of planting fields repeatedly, the essential soil nutrients would have been depleted, producing lower yields, especially with corn crops, and the Cahokians did not grow beans, which would normally reintroduce nitrogen into the soil.

ENVIRONMENTAL DEGRADATION

There is evidence of climate change occurring at different times in the Midwest that may have affected the growth and development of Cahokia and also contributed to its demise. A period of more favorable climate began about the time that Cahokia developed as a major community and continued to about AD 1135. Around that time, a period of drought occurred that lasted for about thirty-five years or more, adding an element of stress to an already fragile economy and political system. The Cahokia elite probably kept granaries stocked with surplus crops from years of good yields to redistribute in times of poor yields or as they saw fit for other purposes, such as trade. As surpluses and yields dwindled due to the droughts, the ability to feed the once massive population weakened. Also, many of the upland support communities were failing at this time, affecting the amount of food being provisioned for Cahokia.

There is also some evidence of a general cooling of the environment beginning in the 1200s and perhaps a shifting of the rainy season away from the growing season, changes that would have affected not only the agricultural crops but also the natural flora and fauna. This was the beginning of an episode that became known as the "Little Ice Age," although the most severe climatic effects did not take place until a couple centuries after Cahokia was abandoned. Nonetheless, there were probably increasing incidents of severe weather, flood and drought, as well as earlier and later frosts that affected Cahokia's food supplies.

POLITICAL CHANGE

Such failures would be seen by the commoners as the responsibility of the ruling elite and priests, who were responsible for ensuring successful crops and supplies and favorable communion with the gods and spiritual forces. As faith in the leadership eroded, there were likely challenges to Cahokia's authority, from within and beyond. Factions would have developed, competing for power and taking Cahokia in a new direction during the Moorehead phase. If there were any weak or bad leaders during this tenuous time, that would also have had a serious effect on the political climate. How leaders were selected is not clear, but most likely the process was based on heredity—usually a son of a previous chief succeeded his father. Many historic tribes are known to have "peace chiefs" and "war chiefs," often with equal authority, depending on the political conditions at the time. This may have been true at Cahokia and is hinted at in the burial of two males as part of the beaded burial at Mound 72.

Rival communities emerged in the river valleys to the south, never equaling Cahokia but at the same time competing for influence and power. People living in the hinterlands abandoned their communities and went elsewhere, perhaps joining some of these rival towns.

A paramount chief of Cahokia and his attendants greet the rising sun from the top of Monks Mound. *Michael Hampshire, Cahokia Mounds State Historic Site.*

WARFARE AND CONFLICT

The threat of conflict is evidenced by the repeated building of the stockade around central Cahokia. At about the same time, many other Mississippian sites, large and small, were being fortified, indicating that warfare had become an integral component of the Mississippian world by AD 1200. Much of the East St. Louis mound group, protected by stockade walls, was demolished by fire. Whether this was a result of accidental fire or attack is not clear, but the archaeologists who dug there believe that it was an attack. At Cahokia, in the areas investigated thus far, there is also no clear evidence of attack, destruction or burning of the walls, but the fact that the wall was built four times in succession indicates that there was a continuing threat. Raids, warfare, burning of towns and other acts of aggression—whether emanating from Cahokia or directed at it—would have destabilized this community and those who had depended on it. This is another factor contributing to its decline.

ECONOMIC DECLINE

For many years, Cahokia was looked at as a trade center, but that concept has been reevaluated in recent years, as most researchers don't see Cahokia as having been based on a market economy. However, Cahokians did engage in long-distance, as well as regional, trade. Gulf Coast and Atlantic marine shells occur in massive quantities as both finished products (beads, cups, gorgets) and the raw material, with at least a dozen species of shell identified, in addition to bead-making workshop areas. Lake Superior copper occurs, but large, finished ritual objects like those found at other Mississippian sites are yet to be found at Cahokia. An exception are the copper staffs at Mound 72. At least one copper workshop area has been identified by Mound 34, so we know that they were processing it into finished prestige goods. Mica from the southern Appalachians occurs sporadically, except for a huge pile of it found at Mound 72. Minerals such as galena and hematite, a number of chert types, salt, Missouri flintclay (used to make ceremonial figurines and pipes), St. Francois Mountains diorite (for making axes) and other resources came from sources within about one hundred miles of Cahokia. Some researchers believe that Cahokia may have had some control in accessing, processing and redistributing these materials or objects made from them,

Disc- and barrel-shaped beads were made from pieces of large whelk shells from the Gulf of Mexico. *Illinois State Museum.*

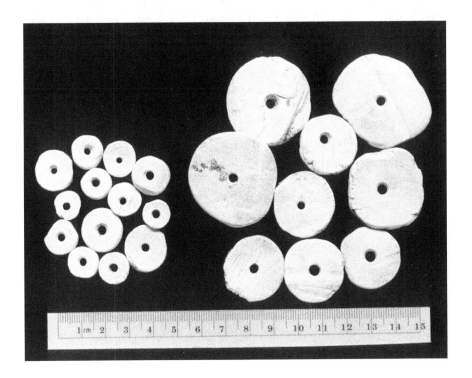

Two views of the Birger Figurine (cast) made from Missouri flintclay, a soft red stone. It depicts a woman hoeing the back of a snake, whose tail then becomes vines, with squashes growing up her back. She represents the earth mother and fertility symbolism. *Cahokia Mounds State Historic Site (original at the University of Illinois).*

but there is disagreement about the amount of control Cahokia had as new polities developed, challenged and interacted with one another and less with Cahokia. As Cahokia's power waned, so did its influence in the trade networks, although it still had access to them. There are suggestions that by the later phases at Cahokia, exotic goods were more accessible to the general population than before and were no longer just in the hands of the elite.

Robert Hall suggests that another economic factor may have been involved—bison hunting. Bison were not present in enough numbers east of the Mississippi to be considered an economic resource until the 1600s, although isolated examples of an earlier presence have been found. However, bison were more common to the west, in the margins of the Great Plains and Eastern Prairie, and after AD 1200 there is archaeological evidence that prehistoric groups in that region were taking more advantage of that resource. It is possible that this became attractive to enough of the Cahokia population to draw them away, especially if the droughts and other climate factors were coming into play.

HEALTH AND DISEASE

With thousands of people living at Cahokia, often in close quarters, the opportunity for the spread of contagious diseases would have increased. Living conditions may not have been ideal; excessive amounts of human and food waste that required disposal, the stagnant waters of the old borrow pits, the miasma of the surrounding swamps and marshes and the smog from countless smoky fires would all have had deleterious effects on the health of the populace. Although few cemeteries have been identified at Cahokia, analyses of those found at other Mississippian sites identify some health and nutritional deficiencies. There was an increase in lung diseases such as tuberculosis, which would have spread easily, and examples of blastomycosis, caused by a soil-borne fungus, have been noted. With all of the earth-moving and farming that occurred at Cahokia, this is not surprising. Nutritionally, an overdependence on corn in the diet can lead to health problems such as iron deficiency anemia. All of these diseases and conditions affect the bones in their later stages of development. There is also an indication of

A Cahokia household grouping of structures and activities. *Lloyd K. Townsend, Cahokia Mounds State Historic Site.*

greater occurrences of dental caries (cavities) and gum diseases with the high-carbohydrate, corn-based diet. Infant mortality rates increased some during Mississippian times, perhaps as infants were weaned earlier onto a corn-mush diet that didn't provide adequate nutrition.

Thus, although Cahokia offered many advantages of the "big city," it may not have been the best place to live. How they handled human waste, for example, is not known. We do know that each household had a number of refuse pits around it, and it is possible that some of these served a "toilet" function. There also may have been neighborhood or community latrines, but none has been identified as such yet. There must have been some mechanism in place to handle this problem, but over time, bacteria and other organisms may have worked their way into water supplies and people's systems. I imagine Cahokia was somewhat odoriferous on a hot summer's day as well.

THE END OF CAHOKIA

Whatever the causes, Cahokia was essentially vacant by the mid-1300s, its people having moved on to other places. Some probably became part of the Oneota tradition that had started earlier in the northern Mississippi Valley and made incursions into the American Bottom area late in prehistory. Others may have become some of the tribes with which we are more familiar. Over the past decade, archaeologists have been leaning more and more to suggesting that some of the central Siouan (Dhegiha) speakers have possible Mississippian connections, and maybe connections with Cahokia itself. The Osage, Omaha, Quapaw, Ponca and Kansa were at one time together in the Mississippi-Ohio confluence area. They split at some unknown time in the past, and the Quapaw went south to Arkansas; the others moved through the Cahokia area, with the Osage and Kansa heading to the Missouri-Mississippi confluence area and eventually up the Missouri to western Missouri and eastern Kansas and the Ponca and Omaha moving even farther up the Missouri into Iowa and South Dakota. Although none of these had mound-building traditions, their complex political and social structures and their iconographies fit well with those of Mississippians, and some of their oral traditions also suggest links to Cahokia.

Someday we may have a more definitive answer to this and numerous other questions as continuing research with traditional and new archaeological techniques at Cahokia proper and related sites near and far will help us understand more about this fascinating place—America's first city.

Conclusion

This book tells only part of the story of Cahokia. As I indicated in the introduction, my focus in this book has been to provide basic information about Cahokia and its primary features. There is much more that is known and discussed elsewhere, but there is still much that we don't know about this great site. Less than 1 percent of the site has been excavated, even though there probably have been close to one hundred excavation projects over the past ninety years.

Of course, there are no plans to totally excavate the site and its mounds, but there are questions we hope to answer with additional research. We know that Cahokia grew from humble beginnings to become a huge urban complex, only to eventually fail much like other cities, states and civilizations around the world. The dynamics of this process are just beginning to be understood, and as more data is accumulated and interpreted, it will expand our knowledge.

We need to understand better the way Cahokia evolved and impacted other Mississippians, near and far. We know its influence was widespread. Red stone figurines made from Missouri flint clay depicting cultural heroes, warriors, earth mothers and empowered animals have been found throughout the Mississippian world. However, they are all believed to have been made at Cahokia and possibly transported by emissaries spreading Cahokia's message, religion and belief system.

What was so special about Cahokia? What was the power of this place that caused it to surpass all others? Was it a charismatic leader, a new religion, its location or some combination of these? We will never know all of the answers, and sometimes the more we dig the more questions we raise. However, continued research is important to learn more about this phenomenon we call Cahokia.

Bibliography

This bibliography includes publications and papers referred to in the preceding text, as well as numerous other publications about or including Cahokia that will be of interest to the general reader and other researchers looking for more details about aspects of Cahokia that may or may not be covered in this manuscript. Some are technical, and others are in a more general format. The bibliographies in each of the following texts will lead readers to other sources as well.

Ahler, Steven R., and Peter J. Depuydt. *A Report on the 1931 Powell Mound Excavations, Madison County, Illinois.* Springfield: Illinois State Museum Reports of Investigations, No. 43., 1987.

Ambrose, Stanley H., Jane Buikstra and Harold W. Krueger. "Status and Gender Differences in Diet at Mound 72, Cahokia, Revealed by Isotopic Analysis of Bone." *Journal of Anthropological Archaeology* 22 (2003): 217–26.

Anderson, James P. "Cahokia Palisade Sequence." In *Explorations Into Cahokia Archaeology*, edited by Melvin L. Fowler. Urbana: Illinois Archaeological Survey, Bulletin No. 7, 1977.

Bareis, Charles J., and James W. Porter, eds. *American Bottom Archaeology.* Urbana: University of Illinois Press, 1984.

Benchley, Elizabeth D. "Summary Report of Excavations on the Southwest Corner of the First Terrace of Monks Mound: 1968, 1969, 1971." In *Cahokia Archaeology: Field Reports*, edited by Melvin L. Fowler. Springfield: Illinois State Museum Research Series, No. 3., 1975.

————. *Summary Report on the Controlled Surface Collections of the Ramey Field, Cahokia Mounds Historic Site in Madison County, Illinois.* Milwaukee: University of Wisconsin–Milwaukee Archaeological Research Laboratory, Report of Investigations No. 51, 1975.

Beck, Robin A., Jr. "Persuasive Politics and Domination at Cahokia and Moundville." In *Leadership and Polity in Mississippian Society*, edited by Brian M. Butler and Paul D. Welch. Occasional Paper No. 33, 19–42. Carbondale: Center for Archaeological Investigations, Southern Illinois University–Carbondale, 2006.

Benson, Larry V., Michael S. Berry, Edward A. Jolie, Jerry D. Spangler, David W. Stahle and Eugene M. Hattori. "Possible Impacts of Early-11th-, middle-12th-, and late-13th-Century Droughts on Western Native Americans and the Mississippians of Cahokia." *Quaternary Science Review* 26 (2007): 336–50.

Brackenridge, Henry. *Views of Louisiana Together with a Journal of a Voyage up the Missouri River in 1811.* Chicago: Quadrangle Books, Inc., 1814. Reprint, 1962.

Brown, James A. "The Cahokia Mound 72 Sub-1 Burials as Collective Representation." *Wisconsin Archaeologist* 84, nos. 1 & 2 (2003): 81–97.

————. "Where's the Power in Mound Building? An Eastern Woodlands Perspective." In *Leadership and Polity in Mississippian Society*, edited by Brian M. Butler and Paul D. Welch. Occasional Paper No. 33. Carbondale: Center for Archeological Investigations, Southern Illinois University–Carbondale, 2006.

Brown, James A., Richard A. Kerber and Howard D. Winters. "Trade and the Evolution of Exchange Relations at the Beginning of the Mississippian Period." In *The Mississippian Emergence*, edited by Bruce D. Smith. N.p.: Smithsonian Institution Press, 1990.

Brown, James, and John Kelly. "Cahokia and the Southeastern Ceremonial Complex." In *Mounds, Modoc, and Mesoamerica, Papers in Honor of Melvin L. Fowler*, edited by Stephen R. Ahler. Springfield: Illinois State Museum Scientific Papers, Vol. 28, 2000.

Bushnell, David I., Jr. *The Cahokia and Surrounding Mound Groups.* Papers of the Peabody Museum of American Archaeology and Ethnology 3(1), 1904. Harvard University Press, Cambridge, Massachusetts.

Butler, Brian M., and Paul D. Welch, eds. *Leadership and Polity in Mississippian Society.* Occasional Paper No. 33. Carbondale: Center for Archaeological Investigations, Southern Illinois University–Carbondale, 2006.

Byers, A. Martin. *Cahokia: A World Renewal Cult Heterarchy*. Gainesville: University Press of Florida, 2006.

Chappel, Sally A. Kitt. *Cahokia: Mirror of the Cosmos*. Chicago: University of Chicago Press, 2002.

Claassen, Cheryl I., and Samuella Sigmann. "Sourcing Busycon Artifacts of the Eastern United States." *American Antiquity* 58, no. 2 (1993): 333–47.

Cobb, Charles R. "Mississippian Chiefdoms: How Complex?" *Annual Review of Anthropology* 32 (2003): 63–84.

Collins, James M. "The Archaeology of the Cahokia Mounds ICT-II: Structures." Illinois Cultural Resources Study No. 10, 1990. Illinois Historic Preservation Agency, Springfield, Illinois.

Collins, James M., and Michael L. Chalfant. "A Second Terrace Perspective on Monks Mound." *American Antiquity* 59, no. 2 (1993): 334–59.

Dalan, Rinita A. "Defining Archaeological Features with Electro-magnetic Surveys at the Cahokia Mounds State Historic Site." *Geophysics* 56, no. 8 (1991): 1280–87.

———. "Electromagnetic Reconnaissance of the Central Palisade at the Cahokia Mounds State Historic Site." *Wisconsin Archaeologist* 70 (1989): 309–32.

———. Geophysical Investigations of the Prehistoric Palisade Sequence. Illinois Cultural Resources Study No. 8, 1989. Illinois Historic Preservation Agency, Springfield, Illinois.

Dalan, Rinita A., George Holley, William Woods, Harold Watters and John Koepke. *Envisioning Cahokia: A Landscape Perspective*. DeKalb: Northern Illinois University Press, 2003.

Dalan, Rinita A., Harold W. Watters Jr., George R. Holley and William I. Woods. "Sixth Annual Cahokia Mounds Field School: Understanding Mound Construction." Manuscript on file at IHPA and Cahokia Mounds, 1994. Office of Contract Archaeology, Southern Illinois University–Edwardsville.

Emerson, Thomas E. *Cahokia and the Archaeology of Power*. Tuscaloosa: University of Alabama Press, 1992.

———. "Cahokia and the Evidence for Late Pre-Columbian War in the North American Midcontinent." In *North American Indigenous Warfare and Ritual Violence*, edited by Richard J. Chacon and Ruben G. Mendoza. Tucson: University of Arizona Press, 2007.

———. "Crossing Boundaries Between Worlds: Changing Beliefs and Mortuary Practices at Cahokia." *Wisconsin Archaeologist* 84, nos. 1 & 2 (2003): 73–80.

———. "The Mississippian Dispersed Village as a Social and Environmental Strategy." In *Late Prehistoric Agriculture: Observations from the Midwest*, edited by William I. Woods. Springfield: Studies in Illinois Archaeology No. 8, Illinois Historic Preservation Agency, 1992.

———. *Mississippian Stone Images in Illinois*. Urbana: Illinois Archaeological Survey, Circular No. 6, 1982.

Emerson, Thomas E., Brad Koldehoff and Timothy R. Pauketat. "Serpents, Female Deities, and Fertility: Symbolism in the Early Cahokia Countryside." In *Mounds, Modoc, and Mesoamerica, Papers in Honor of Melvin L. Fowler*. Springfield: Illinois State Museum Scientific Papers, Vol. 28, 2000.

Emerson, Thomas E., and Randall E. Hughes. "Figurines, Flint Clay Sourcing, the Ozark Highlands and Cahokian Acquisition." *American Antiquity* 65, no. 1 (2000): 79–101.

Emerson, Thomas E., Randall E. Hughes, Mary R. Hynes and Sarah U. Wisseman. "The Sourcing and Interpretation of Cahokia-Style Figurines in the Trans-Mississippi South and Southeast." *American Antiquity* 68, no. 2 (2003): 287–313.

Emerson, Thomas E., and R. Barry Lewis, eds. *Cahokia and the Hinterlands: Middle Mississippian Cultures of the Midwest*. Urbana: University of Illinois Press, 1991.

Fortier, Andrew C., ed. *The Archaeology of the East St. Louis Mound Center, Part II: Transportation*. Archaeological Research Reports, No. 22. Illinois Transportation Archaeological Research Program, University of Illinois at Urbana-Champaign, 2007.

Fortier, Andrew C., and Dale L. McElrath. "Deconstructing the Emergent Mississippian Concept: The Case for the Terminal Late Woodland in the American Bottom." *Midcontinental Journal of Archaeology* 27, no. 2 (2002): 171–215.

Fowler, Melvin L. "The Ancient Skies and Skywatchers of Cahokia: Woodhenges, Eclipses, and Cahokian Cosmology." *Wisconsin Archaeologist* 77, no. 3–4 (1996).

———. "Cahokia: Ancient Capitol of the Midwest." Addison-Wesley Module in Anthropology No. 48. Reading, IL: Addison Wesley Publishing Co., 1974.

———. "Cahokia and the American Bottom: Settlement Archaeology." In *Mississippian Settlement Patterns*, edited by Bruce D. Smith. New York: Academic Press, 1978.

———. *The Cahokia Atlas: A Historical Atlas of Cahokia Archaeology*. Revised edition. Urbana: University of Illinois Press, 1997.

———. "Cahokia: Circles, Calendars, Corn and Cosmology." *Wisconsin Archaeologist* 84, nos. 1 & 2 (2003): 55–71.

———. "A Precolumbian Urban Center on the Mississippi." *Scientific American* 26, no. 2 (August 1975): 92–101.

Fowler, Melvin L., ed. *Cahokia Archaeology: Field Reports.* Springfield: Illinois State Museum Research Series No. 3, n.d.

———. *Explorations into Cahokia Archaeology.* Urbana: Illinois Archaeological Survey Bulletin No. 7, 1969. Revised 1973, 1977.

Fowler, Melvin L., and James P. Anderson. "Report on 1971 Excavations at Mound 72, Cahokia Mounds State Park." In *Cahokia Archaeology: Field Reports*, edited by Melvin L. Fowler. Papers in Anthropology 3, 1975. Illinois State Museum, Springfield, Illinois.

Fowler, Melvin L., Jerome Rose, Barbara Vander Leest and Steven R. Ahler. *The Mound 72 Area: Dedicated and Sacred Space in Early Cahokia.* Reports of Investigations No. 54, 1999. Illinois State Museum Society, Springfield, Illinois.

Fritz, Gayle J. "'Newer,' 'Better' Maize and the Mississippian Emergence: A Critique of Prime Mover Explanations." In *Late Prehistoric Agriculture: Observations from the Midwest*, edited by William I. Woods. Studies in Illinois Archaeology No. 8, 1992. Illinois Historic Preservation Agency, Springfield, Illinois.

Goldstein, Lynne. "Mississippian Ritual as Viewed through the Practice of Secondary Disposal of the Dead." In *Mounds, Modoc, and Mesoamerica, Papers in Honor of Melvin L. Fowler*, edited by Steven R. Ahler. Springfield: Illinois State Museum Scientific Papers, Vol. 28, 2000.

Green, William, and Roland L. Rodeel. "The Mississippian Presence and Cahokia Interaction at Trempeleau, Wisconsin." *American Antiquity* 59, no. 2 (1994): 334–59.

Gregg, Michael D. "A Population Estimate for Cahokia." In *Perspectives in Cahokia Archaeology*, edited by James A. Brown. Urbana: Illinois Archaeological Survey Bulletin No. 10, 1975.

Griffin, James B. "Cahokia Interaction with Contemporary Southeastern and Eastern Societies." *Midcontinental Journal of Archaeology* 18 (1985): 3–17.

Hall, Robert L. *An Archaeology of the Soul: North American Indian Belief and Ritual.* Urbana: University of Illinois Press, 1997.

———. "Chronology and Phases at Cahokia." In *Perspectives in Cahokia Archaeology*, edited by James Brown. Urbana: Illinois Archaeological Survey Bulletin No. 10, 1975.

———. "The Cultural Background of Mississippian Symbolism." In *The Southeastern Ceremonial Complex*, edited by Patricia Galloway. Lincoln: University of Nebraska Press, 1989.

———. "Exploring the Mississippian Big Bang at Cahokia." In *A Pre-Columbian World*, edited by Jeffrey Quilter and Mary Miller. Washington, D.C.: Dumbarton Oaks, 2006.

———. "Sacred Foursomes and Green Corn Ceremonialism." In *Mounds, Modoc, and Mesoamerica, Papers in Honor of Melvin L. Fowler*. Springfield: Illinois State Museum Scientific Papers, vol. 28, 2000.

Harn, Alan D. "Cahokia and the Mississippian Emergence in the Spoon River Area of Illinois." *Transactions of the Illinois Academy of Science* 68 (1975): 414–34.

Holley, George R. *Archaeology of the Cahokia Mounds ICT-II: Ceramics*. Illinois Cultural Resources Study 11. Springfield: Illinois Historic Preservation Agency, 1987.

———. " Microliths and the Kunnemann Tract: An Assessment of Craft Production at the Cahokia Site." *Illinois Archaeology* 7, nos. 1 & 2 (1995).

Holley, George R., and John A. Koepke. "Harmony in the Cahokian World." *Wisconsin Archaeologist* 84, nos. 1 & 2 (2003): 155–64.

Holley, George R., Neal H. Lopinot, William I. Woods and John E. Kelly. "Dynamics of Community Organization at Prehistoric Cahokia." In *Households and Communities: Proceedings of the 21st Annual Chacmool Conference*, edited by Scott MacEachern, David J.W. Archer and Richard D. Gavin. Calgary, AB, 1989.

Holley, George R., R.A. Dalan and H.W. Watters Jr. "Investigations at the West Borrow Pit Group, Cahokia Mounds State Historic Site." Manuscript on file at IHPA and Cahokia Mounds, 1996. Office of Contract Archaeology, Southern Illinois University–Edwardsville.

Holley, George R., Rinita A. Dalan, Harold W. Watters Jr. and Julie N. Harper. "Investigations at the Tippetts Mound Group, Cahokia Mounds State Historic Site." Manuscript on file at IHPA and Cahokia Mounds State Historic Site, 1995. Office of Contract Archaeology, Southern Illinois University–Edwardsville.

Holley, George R., Rinita Dalan and Philip A. Smith. "Investigations in the Cahokia Site Grand Plaza." *American Antiquity* 58, no. 2 (1993): 306–19.

Holley, George R., and Stephen L. Lekson. "Comparing Southwestern and Southeastern Great Towns." In *Great Towns and Regional Polities in the Prehistoric American Southwest and Southeast*, edited by Jill E. Neitzel. Albuquerque: University of New Mexico Press, 1999.

Holt, Julie Zimmerman. "Rethinking the Ramey State: Was Cahokia the Center of a Theater State?" *American Antiquity* 74, no. 2 (2009): 231–54.

Iseminger, William R. "Cahokia, a Mississippian Metropolis." *Central States Archaeological Journal* 33, no. 4 (1986): 228–45.

———. "Culture and Environment in the American Bottom: The Rise and Fall of Cahokia Mounds." In *Common Fields: An Environmental History of St. Louis*, edited by Andrew Hurley. St. Louis: Missouri Historical Society Press, 1997.

———. "Excavations at Cahokia Mounds." *Archaeology* 39, no. 1 (1986): 58–59.

———. "Mighty Cahokia." *Archaeology* 49, no. 3 (1996): 30–37.

———. "The Monks of Cahokia." In *Highways to the Past: Essays on Illinois Archaeology in Honor of Charles J. Bareis*. Illinois Archaeology, vol. 5, nos. 1 and 2. Urbana: Illinois Archaeological Survey, 1993.

———. "Monks Mound: A 'Moving' Monument." *Historic Illinois* 20, no. 2 (1997).

———. "Prehistoric Cultures at the Confluence and the Rise and Fall of Cahokia Mounds." Paper presented at the Before Lewis and Clark Symposium, April 5, 2001, St. Louis, Missouri.

Iseminger, William R., George R. Holley, et al. *The Archaeology of the Cahokia Palisade*. Illinois Cultural Resources Study No. 14. Springfield: Illinois Historic Preservation Agency, 1990.

Iseminger, William R., and John E. Kelly. "Partitioning the Sacred Precinct." *Cahokian* 3, no. 5 (Summer 1995).

Jeske, Robert J. "World Systems Theory, Core Periphery Interactions and Elite Economic Exchange in Mississippian Societies." *Journal of World-Systems Research* 2 (1999).

Kelly, John E. "The Archaeology of the East St. Louis Mound Center: Past and Present." *Illinois Archaeology* 6 (1994): 1–57.

———. "The Context of the Post Pit and Meaning of the Sacred Pole at the East St. Louis Mound Group." *Wisconsin Archaeologist* 84, nos. 1 & 2 (2003): 107–25.

———. "East St. Louis's Lost Legacy: The Rediscovery of an Urban Mound Center." *Gateway Heritage* 20, no. 1 (1999): 4–15.

———. "The Emergence of Mississippian Culture in the American Bottom Region." In *The Mississippian Emergence*, edited by Bruce Smith. Washington, D.C.: Smithsonian Institution Press, 1990.

———. "Formative Developments at Cahokia and the Adjacent American Bottom: A Merrell Tract Perspective." PhD diss., University of Wisconsin-

Madison, 1980. [Published by the Archaeological Research Laboratory, Western Illinois University–Macomb, 2 vols., 1982.]

———. "The Impact of Maize on the Development of Nucleated Settlements: An American Bottom Example." In *Late Prehistoric Agriculture: Observations from the Midwest*, edited by William I. Woods. Studies in Illinois Archaeology No. 8. Springfield: Illinois Historic Preservation Agency, 1992.

———. "The Nature and Context of Emergent Mississippian Cultural Dynamics in the Greater American Bottom." In *Late Woodland Societies: Tradition and Transformation Across the Midcontinent*, edited by Thomas E. Emerson, Dale L. McElrath and Andrew C. Fortier. Lincoln: University of Nebraska Press, 2000.

———. "The Public Architecture on the Merrell Tract, Cahokia." Report submitted to the Cahokia Mounds Museum Society, December 10, 1996.

———. "The Ritualization of Cahokia: The Structure and Organization of Early Cahokia Crafts." In *Leadership and Polity in Mississippian Society*, edited by Brian M. Butler and Paul D. Welch. Occasional Paper 33. Carbondale: Center for Archaeological Investigations, Southern Illinois University–Carbondale, 2006.

Kelly, John E., and James A. Brown. "Cahokia: The Process and Principles of the Creation of an Early Mississippian City." Paper presented at the Annual Meeting of the Society for American Archaeology, 2009, Atlanta, Georgia.

Kelly, John E., James A. Brown, Jenna M. Hamlin, Lucretia S. Kelly, Laura Kozuch, Kathryn Parker and Julieann Van Nest. "Mound 34: The Context for the Early Evidence of the Southeastern Ceremonial Complex at Cahokia." In *Chronology, Iconography, and Style: Current Perspectives on the Social and Temporal Contexts of the Southeastern Ceremonial Complex*, edited by Adam King. Tuscaloosa: University of Alabama Press, 2007.

Kelly, John E., James A. Brown and Lucretia S. Kelly. "The Context of Religion at Cahokia: The Mound 34 Case." In *Religion in the Material World*, edited by Lars Foeglin. Center for Archaeological Investigations Occasional Paper No. 36. Carbondale: Southern Illinois University–Carbondale, 2008.

Kelly, John E., Timothy Schilling, Neal Lopinot and T.R. Kidder. "New Perspectives on an Old Monument." Paper presented at the Annual Meeting of the Illinois Archaeological Survey, September 26, 2009, Springfield, Illinois.

Kelly, Lucretia S. *Animal Resource Exploitation by the Early Cahokia Populations on the Merrell Tract.* Urbana: Illinois Archaeological Survey Circular No. 4, 1979.

———. "A Case of Ritual Feasting at the Cahokia Site." In *Feasts: Archaeological and Ethnographic Perspectives on Food, Politics, and Power,* edited by Michael Dietler and Brian Hayden. Washington, D.C.: Smithsonian Institution Press, 2001.

Klepinger, Linda L. "The Skeletons of Fingerhut: An Early Cahokia Cemetery." *Illinois Archaeology* 5, nos. 1 & 2 (1993).

Knight, Vernon James, Jr. "The Institutional Organization of Mississippian Religion." *American Antiquity* 51, no. 4 (1986): 675–87.

Koldehoff, Brad. "The Cahokia Flake Tool Industry: Socioeconomic Implications for Late Prehistory in the Central Mississippi Valley." In *The Organization of Core Technology,* edited by J. Johnson and C. Morrow. Boulder, CO: Westview Press, 1987.

Koldehoff, Brad, Charles O. Witty and Mike Kolb. "Recent Investigations in the Vicinity of Mounds 27 and 28 at Cahokia: The Yale Avenue Borrow Pit." *Illinois Archaeology* 12, nos. 1 & 2 (2000).

Lewis, R. Barry, and Charles Stout, eds. *Mississippian Towns and Sacred Spaces: Searching for an Architectural Grammar.* Tuscaloosa: University of Alabama Press, 1998.

Lopinot, Neal H. "A New Crop of Data on the Cahokian Polity." In *Agricultural Origins and Development in the Midcontinent,* edited by W. Green. Iowa City, IA: Office of the State Archaeologist, Report 19, 1994.

Lopinot, Neal H., Alan J. Brown and George R. Holley. "Archaeological Investigations on the Western Periphery of the Cahokia Site." *Illinois Archaeology* 5, nos. 1 & 2 (1993).

Lopinot, Neal H., Lucretia S. Kelly, George R. Milner and Richard Paine. *The Archaeology of the Cahokia Mounds ICT-II: Biological Remains.* Illinois Cultural Resources Study No. 13. Springfield: Illinois Historic Preservation Agency, 1991.

Lopinot, Neal H., and William I. Woods. "Wood Overexploitation and the Collapse of Cahokia." In *Foraging and Farming in the Eastern Woodlands,* edited by C. Margaret Scarry. Gainesville: University Press of Florida, 1993.

McGimsey, Charles R., and Michael D. Wiant. *Limited Archaeological Investigations at Monks Mound (11-Ms38): Some Perspectives on Its Stability, Structure, and Age.* Springfield: Illinois Historic Preservation Agency Studies in Illinois Archaeology No. 1, 1984.

Mehrer, Mark W. *Cahokia's Countryside: Household Archaeology, Settlement Patterns, and Social Power.* Dekalb: Northern Illinois University Press, 1995.

Mehrer, Mark, and James M. Collins. "Household Archaeology at Cahokia and in Its Hinterlands." In *Mississippian Development in the Midcontinent.* Iowa City: Report 19, Office of the State Archaeologist, University of Iowa, 1995.

Milner, George R. "Archaeological Indicators of Rank in the Cahokia Chiefdom." In *Theory, Method and Practice in Modern Archaeology*, edited by Robert J. Jeske and Douglas K. Charles. Westport, IL: Praeger Publishers, 2003.

———. *The Cahokia Chiefdom.* Washington, D.C.: Smithsonian Institution Press, 1998.

———. "Development and Dissolution of a Mississippian Society in the American Bottom, Illinois." In *Political Structure and Change in the Prehistoric Southeastern United States*, edited by John F. Scarry. Gainesville: University Press of Florida, 1996.

———. "Health and Culture Change in the Late Prehistoric American Bottom, Illinois." In *What Mean These Bones? Southeastern Bioarchaeology*, edited by M.L. Powell. Tuscaloosa: University of Alabama Press, 1992.

———. "The Late Prehistoric Cahokia Cultural System of the Mississippi River Valley: Foundations, Fluorescence and Fragmentation." *Journal of World Prehistory* 4, no. 1 (1990): 1–43.

———. *The Moundbuilders: Ancient Peoples of Eastern North America.* London: Thames and Hudson, Ltd., 2003.

Milner, George R., and Sissel Schroeder. "Mississippian Sociopolitical Systems." In *Great Towns and Regional Polities in the Prehistoric American Southwest and Southeast*, edited by Jill E. Neitzel. Albuquerque: University of New Mexico Press, 1999.

Mink, Claudia G. *Cahokia: City of the Sun.* Collinsville, IL: Cahokia Mounds Museum Society, 1992.

Moorehead, Warren K. *The Cahokia Mounds.* Edited by and with an introduction by John E. Kelly. Classics in Southeastern Archaeology Series. Tuscaloosa: University of Alabama Press, 2000.

Muller, Jon. *Mississippian Political Economy.* New York: Plenum Press, 1997.

———. "Southeastern Interaction and Integration." In *Great Towns and Regional Polities in the Prehistoric American Southwest and Southeast*, edited by Jill E. Neitzel. Albuquerque: University of New Mexico Press, 1999.

Neitzel, Jill E., ed. *Great Towns and Regional Polities in the Prehistoric American Southwest and Southeast.* Albuquerque: University of New Mexico Press, 1999.

O'Brien, Patricia J. "Cahokia: The Political Capital of the 'Ramey' State?" *North American Archaeologist* 25 (1989): 188–97.

———. "Early State Economics: Cahokia, Capital of the Ramey State." In *Early State Economics*, edited by Henri J.M. Claessen and Pieter van de Velde. Brunswick, IL: Transaction Publishers, 1991.

———. *A Formal Analysis of Cahokia Ceramics from the Powell Tract*. Urbana: Illinois Archaeological Survey Monograph No. 3, 1972.

———. "Prehistoric Politics: Petroglyphs and the Political Boundaries of Cahokia." *Gateway Heritage* 15, no. 1 (1994).

———. "Urbanism, Cahokia, and Middle Mississippian." *Archaeology* 25, no. 3 (1972): 188–97.

O'Brien, Patricia, and W. McHugh. "Mississippian Solstice Shrines and a Cahokian Calendar: An Hypothesis Based on Ethnohistory and Archaeology." *North American Archaeologist* 8, no. 3 (1987): 227–47.

Pauketat, Timothy R. "America's Ancient Warriors." *Military History Quarterly* (Summer 1999): 50–55.

———. *Ancient Cahokia and the Mississippians*. London: Cambridge University Press, 2004.

———. *The Archaeology of Downtown Cahokia: The Tract 15-A and Dunham Tract Excavations*. Studies in Archaeology No. 1, Illinois Transportation Archaeology Research Program. Urbana: University of Illinois, 1998.

———. *The Ascent of Chiefs: Cahokia and Mississippian Politics in Native North America*. Tuscaloosa: University of Alabama Press, 1994.

———. *Cahokia: Ancient America's Great City on the Mississippi*. New York: Penguin Library of American Indian History, 2009.

———. *Chiefdoms and Other Archaeological Delusions*. Lanham, MD: AltaMira Press, 2007.

———. "Founders Cults and the Archaeology of Wa-kan-da." In *Memory Work: Archaeologies of Material Practices*, edited by Barbara J. Mills and William H. Walker. Santa Fe, NM: School for Advanced Research Advanced Seminar Series, 2008.

———. "A Fourth Generation Synthesis of Cahokia and Mississippianization." *Midcontinental Journal of Archaeology* 27, no. 2 (2002): 149–70.

———. "Preliminary Observations of Building Density at Cahokia's Tract 15A and Dunham Tract." *Illinois Archaeology* 5, nos. 1 & 2 (1993): 402–6.

———. "Refiguring the Archaeology of Greater Cahokia." *Journal of Archaeological Research* 6, no. 1 (1998).

———. "The Reign and Ruin of the Lords of Cahokia: A Dialectic of Dominance." In *Lords of the Southeast: Social Inequality and the Native Elites of Southeastern North America*, edited by A.W. Baker and T.R. Pauketat. Washington, D.C.: American Anthropological Association, Archaeological Papers No. 3, 1992.

———. "Resettled Farmers and the Making of a Mississippian Polity." *American Antiquity* 68, no. 1 (2003): 39–66.

———. "Specialization, Political Symbols and the Crafty Elite of Cahokia." *Southeastern Archaeology* 16, no. 1 (1997).

———. *Temples for Cahokia Lords: Preston Holder's 1955–56 Excavations of the Kunnemann Mound*. Ann Arbor: Museum of Anthropology, University of Michigan, Memoirs No. 26, 1993.

Pauketat, Timothy R., ed. *The Archaeology of the East St. Louis Mound Center*. Part I: *The Southside Excavations*. Transportation Archaeological Research Reports No. 21, Illinois Transportation Archaeological Research Program. Urbana-Champaign: University of Illinois, 2009.

Pauketat, Timothy R., and Alex W. Baker. "Mounds 65 and 66 at Cahokia: Additional Details of the 1927 Excavations." In *Mounds, Modoc, and Mesoamerica, Papers in Honor of Melvin L. Fowler*, edited by Steven R. Ahler. Springfield: Illinois State Museum Scientific Papers, vol. 28, 2000.

Pauketat, Timothy R., Lucretia S. Kelly, Gayle J. Fritz, Neal H. Lopinot, Scott Elias and Eve Hargrave. "The Residues of Feasting and Public Ritual in Early Cahokia." *American Antiquity* 67, no. 2 (2002).

Pauketat, Timothy R., and Thomas E. Emerson. "Representations of Hegemony as Community at Cahokia." In *Material Symbols: Culture and Economy in Prehistory*, edited by John E. Robb. Occasional Paper No 26. Carbondale: Center for Archaeological Investigations, Southern Illinois University–Carbondale, 1999.

Pauketat, Timothy R., and Thomas E. Emerson, eds. *Cahokia: Domination and Ideology in the Mississippian World*. Lincoln: University of Nebraska Press, 1997.

Perino, Gregory. "Recent Information from Cahokia and its Satellites." *Central States Archaeological Journal* 6, no. 4 (1959): 130–38.

Porter, James W. "The Mitchell Site and Prehistoric Exchange Systems at Cahokia." In *Explorations into Cahokia Archaeology*, edited by Melvin Fowler. Urbana: Illinois Archaeological Survey Bulletin No. 7, 1977.

Porubcan, Paul J. "Human and Nonhuman Surplus Display at Mound 72, Cahokia." In *Mounds, Modoc, and Mesoamerica, Papers in Honor of Melvin*

L. Fowler, edited by Steven R. Ahler. Springfield: Illinois State Museum Scientific Papers, vol. 28, 2000.

Reed, Nelson A. "Excavations on the Third Terrace and Front Ramp of Monks Mound, Cahokia: A Personal Narrative." *Illinois Archaeology* 21 (2009).

———. "Monks and Other Mississippian Mounds." In *Explorations into Cahokia Archaeology*, edited by Melvin Fowler. Urbana: Illinois Archaeological Survey Bulletin No. 7, 1977.

Reed, Nelson A., John W. Bennett and James W. Porter. "Solid Core Drilling of Monks Mound: Technique and Findings." *American Antiquity* 33, no. 2 (1968): 137–48.

Reilly, F. Kent, III, and James F. Garber, eds. *Ancient Objects and Sacred Realms: Interpretations of Mississippian Iconography*, with a foreword by Vincas P. Steponaitas. Austin: University of Texas Press, 2007.

Rogers, J. Daniel, and Bruce Smith, eds. *Mississippian Communities and Households*. Tuscaloosa: University of Alabama Press, 1995.

Rolingson, Martha A. "Elements of Community Design at Cahokia." *Wisconsin Archaeologist* 77, nos. 3 & 4 (1996): 84–96.

Salzer, Robert. "Excavations at the Merrell Tract of the Cahokia Site: Summary Field Report, 1973." In *Cahokia Archaeology: Field Reports*, edited by Melvin Fowler. Springfield: Illinois State Museum Research Series No. 3, 1975.

Schilling, Timothy. "Probabilistic History: Modeling the Construction of Monks Mound." Paper presented at the Midwest Archaeological Conference, 2008, Milwaukee, Wisconsin.

———. "Report on Soil Coring in the Vicinity of Monks Mound." Report submitted to the IHPA and Cahokia Mounds State Historic Site, 2009.

Schroeder, Sissel. "Power and Place: Agency, Ecology, and History in the American Bottom, Illinois." *Antiquity* 78 (2004): 812–27.

———. "Settlement Patterns and Cultural Ecology in the Southern American Bottom." In *Mounds, Modoc, and Mesoamerica, Papers in Honor of Melvin L. Fowler*, edited by Steven R. Ahler. Springfield: Illinois State Museum Scientific Papers, vol. 28, 2000.

Sherrod, Clay P., and Martha Ann Rolingson. *Surveyors of the Ancient Mississippi Valley: Modules and Alignments in Prehistoric Mound Sites*. Fayetteville: Arkansas Archaeological Survey Research Series No. 28, 1987.

Skele, Mikels. *The Great Knob: Interpretations of Monks Mound*. Springfield: Illinois Historic Preservation Agency Studies in Archaeology No. 4, 1988.

Smith, Bruce. "Mississippian Elites and Solar Alignments: A Reflection of Managerial Necessity, or Levers of Social Inequality?" In *Lords of the*

Southeast: Social Inequality and the Native Elites of Southeastern North America, edited by A.W. Barker and T.R. Pauketat. Washington, D.C.: Archaeological Papers of the American Anthropological Association 3, 1992.

Smith, Bruce, ed. *Mississippian Settlement Patterns*. New York: Academic Press, 1978.

Smith, Harriet. "The Murdock Mound." In *Explorations Into Cahokia Archaeology*, edited by Melvin Fowler. Urbana: Illinois Archaeological Survey Bulletin No. 7, 1977.

Smith, Michael E. "The Earliest Cities." In *Urban Life: Readings in the Anthropology of the City*, edited by George Gmetch and Walter Zenner. Prospect Heights, IL: Waveland Press, 2002.

Stoltman. James B. "A Reconsideration of the Cultural Processes Linking Cahokia to its Northern Hinterlands During the Period AD 1000–1200." In *Mounds, Modoc, and Mesoamerica, Papers in Honor of Melvin L. Fowler*. Springfield: Illinois State Museum Scientific Papers, vol. 28, 2000.

Stoltman, James B., ed. *New Perspectives on Cahokia: Views from the Periphery*. Monographs in World Archaeology No. 2. Madison, WI: Prehistory Press, 1991.

Stuart, Gene. *Americas Ancient Cities*. Washington, D.C.: National Geographic Society Books, 1988.

Stuart, George C. "Who Were the 'Mound Builders?'" *National Geographic* 142, no. 5 (December 1972): 783–801.

Townsend, Richard F., ed. *Hero, Hawk, and Open Hand: American Indian Art of the Ancient Midwest and South*. Chicago: Art Institute of Chicago in association with Yale University Press, 2004.

Trocolli, Ruth. "Mississippian Chiefs: Women and Men of Power." In *The Dynamics of Power*, edited by Mary O'Donovan. Occasional Paper No. 30, 168–87. Carbondale: Center for Archaeological Investigations, Southern Illinois University–Carbondale, 2002.

Trubitt, Mary Beth. "Mississippian Period Warfare and Palisade Construction at Cahokia." In *Theory, Method, and Practice in Modern Archaeology*, edited by Robert J. Jeske and Douglas K. Charles. Westport, IL: Praeger Publishers, 2003.

———. "Mound Building and Prestige Goods Exchange: Changing Strategies in the Cahokia Chiefdom." *American Antiquity* 65, no. 4 (2000): 669–90.

Tuttle, Martitia P., Eugene S. Schweig, John D. Sims, Robert H. Lafferty, Lorraine W. Wolf and Marion L. Haynes. "The Earthquake Potential of the New Madrid Seismic Zone." *Bulletin of the Seismological Society of America* 92, no. 6 (2002): 2080–89.

Vogel, Joseph O. "Trends in Cahokia Ceramics: Preliminary Study of the Collections from Tracts 15A & 15B." In *Perspectives in Cahokia Archaeology*, edited by James A. Brown. Urbana: Illinois Archaeological Survey Bulletin No. 10, 1975.

Walthall, John A., and Elizabeth D. Benchley. *The River L'Abbe Mission.* Springfield: Illinois Historic Preservation Agency, Studies in Illinois Archaeology No. 2, 1987.

Watson, Robert J. "Sacred Landscapes at Cahokia: Mound 72 and the Mound 72 Precinct." In *Mounds, Modoc, and Mesoamerica, Papers in Honor of Melvin L. Fowler.* Springfield: Illinois State Museum Scientific Papers, vol. 28, 2000.

Welch, Paul D., and Brian M. Butler. "Borne on a Litter with Much Prestige." In *Leadership and Polity in Mississippian Society*, edited by Brian M. Butler and Paul D. Welch. Occasional Paper No. 33. Carbondale: Center for Archaeological Investigations, Southern Illinois University–Carbondale, 2006.

Williams, Kenneth. "Preliminary Summation of Excavations at the East Lobes of Monks Mound." In *Cahokia Archaeology: Field Reports*, edited by Melvin Fowler. Springfield: Illinois State Museum Research Series No. 3, 1975.

Wilson, Gregory D., Jon Marcoux and Brad Koldehoff. "Square Pegs in Round Holes: Organizational Diversity Between Early Moundville and Cahokia." In *Leadership and Polity in Mississippian Society*, edited by Brian M. Butler and Paul D. Welch. Occasional Paper No. 33. Carbondale: Center for Archaeological Investigations, Southern Illinois University–Carbondale, 2006.

Wittry, Warren L. "The American Woodhenge." In *Explorations into Cahokia Archaeology*, edited by Melvin Fowler. Urbana: Illinois Archaeological Survey Bulletin No. 7, 1977.

———. "Cahokia Woodhenge Update." *Archaeoastronomy* 3 (1980): 12–14.

Witty, Charles O. "The Fingerhut Site (11S34/7) Cemetery Three Decades Later." *Illinois Archaeology* 5, nos. 1 & 2 (1993).

Woods, William I. "Monks Mound Revisited." *Terra 2000, Eighth International Conference on the Study and Conservation of Earthen Structures.* May 2000, Torquay, Devon, United Kingdom.

———."Population Nucleation, Intensive Agriculture, and Environmental Degradation: The Cahokia Example." *Agriculture and Human Values* 21 (2004): 255–61.

Woods, William I., ed. *Late Prehistoric Agriculture: Observations from the Midwest.* Studies in Illinois Archaeology No. 8. Springfield: Illinois Historic Preservation Agency, 1992.

Woods, William I., and George R. Holley. "Appendix 3: Current Research at the Cahokia Site (1984–1989)." In *The Cahokia Atlas: A Historical Atlas of Cahokia Archaeology*, by Melvin L. Fowler. Studies in Illinois Archaeology 6. Springfield: Illinois Historic Preservation Agency, 1989. Revised, Urbana: University of Illinois Press, 1997.

Woods, William I., Rodney C. DeMott, Derrick J. Marcucci, Joyce A. Williams and Bonnie L. Gums. *The Archaeology of the Cahokia Mounds ICT-II: Testing and Lithics*. Illinois Cultural Resources Study No. 9. Springfield: Illinois Historic Preservation Agency, 1993.

Young, Biloine. "A Day in Cahokia—AD 1030." In *I Wish I'd Been There*, edited by Bryon Hollinshead. New York: American Historical Publications, Doubleday Publishing, 2006.

Young, Biloine Whiting, and Melvin L. Fowler. *Cahokia: The Great Native American Metropolis*. Urbana: University of Illinois Press, 2000.

About the Author

William R. Iseminger was born in Bloomington, Illinois, and grew up in Arlington, Virginia. He majored in anthropology in college, receiving his BA from the University of Oklahoma and his MA from Southern Illinois University at Carbondale. He participated in excavations in South Dakota and several locations in Illinois, and he has worked at the Cahokia site full time since 1971. He directed  public archaeological field schools for many years and serves as assistant site manager in charge of exhibits, interpretation and public relations at Cahokia for the Illinois Historic Preservation Agency.

Visit us at
www.historypress.net

CPSIA information can be obtained
at www.ICGtesting.com
Printed in the USA
LVHW050742080622
720763LV00006B/461